Caring in the Community: A Networking Approach to Community Partnership

STEVE TREVILLION

CARING IN THE COMMUNITY: A NETWORKING APPROACH TO
COMMUNITY PARTNERSHIP

Published by Longman Group UK Ltd, Westgate House, The High,
Harlow,
Essex CM20 1YR, UK.
Telephone: (0279) 442601
Fax: (0279) 444501
Telex: 81491 Padlog

First published 1992

**A catalogue record for this book is available from the British
Library**

ISBN 0–582–10021–6

Printed in Malaysia by TCP

Contents

1 Social workers and Social networks   6

This book begins with an analysis of how the social network concept can help social workers bring new insights to bear on familiar problems and lead to an interactional and situational approach to the making of community partnership. Ways of defining community partnership in network terms are explored alongside the practical significance particular patterns of *linkage* may have in relation to issues such as isolation, empowerment and access to formal and informal social support.

2 Community partnership: practices and processes   22

In this chapter the theme of community partnership as network process is developed by looking at how networkers can help to develop and sustain patterns of partnership. It is argued that networking is an enabling strategy concerned with interpersonal relationships, community processes, flexibility and informality, communication, and the mobilisation of action-sets. Examples are drawn from the work of social workers and other professionals, and from self-help networking.

3 Patch Social Work: Networking the neighbourhood   38

The next five chapters look at the application of networking principles. Chapter Three, looks at patch social work as a form of neighbourhood networking; Chapter Four, looks at inter-agency networking; Chapter Five, looks at network therapy; Chapter Six, looks at case management and community care; and Chapter Seven looks at self-help and self-advocacy. The diversity of these practices is recognised but it is also made clear that they can all be described in terms of the five practice principles outlined in chapter two.

7 Self-help, self-Advocacy and empowerment

8 Networkers as community brokers   **98**

This chapter argues that although networkers engage in a very varied set of activities all of them are associated with a certain role, that of *community broker:* someone who helps to form a community by bringing individuals, groups or organisations together. An attempt is then made to analyse networking skills in relation to the demands of this mediating role. It is also suggested that the concept of the *community broker* can form the basis of an integrated approach to networking. This leads to a discussion of the concept of systems brokerage or the role community brokers can play in integrating systems such as community care.

9 Community assessment: a networking approach 110

This chapter looks at the implications a networking approach may have for our understanding of what an assessment is, and how one should go about assessing a situation in terms of client need and the potential for community partnership. A number of questions about engagement, negotiation and conflicting perceptions of need are asked and answered. Throughout, the concept of an assessment partnership is developed.

10 Networking with children and adults 123

This final chapter tries to draw together many of the themes of the book by looking in some detail at the way networking might influence or permeate a particular branch of social work. Work with children and families is used to show how networking can help us develop the kind of child centred practice to which the social work profession has long been committed in principle, but which it has often failed to achieve in practice.

Acknowledgements

My thanks to the following people who all in different ways helped to make this book possible:

Suneel Chadha for a very helpful discussion about anti-racist networks,

Clive Turner for finding time to talk to me about the patch social work approach to HIV and AIDS,

Justine Pepperrell for giving me a lot of useful information about Women's Health Network,

Alison Partridge for sharing with me the results of her research on children leaving care,

John Pitts West London Institute of Higher Education — who helped me to get this book published.

My other colleagues in the Social Work Department at West London Institute of Higher Education for their support and encouragement when I felt most uncertain about the value of what I was writing.

Fenella Trevillion for putting up with me while I was writing this book and networking tirelessly to help me gather the information I needed to write it.

Rachel and Phillip for keeping me sane and for understanding that there were times when I could not play with them because I was writing this book.

Introduction

Emergence of a new practice

Case management, multidisciplinary teamwork, the debate about citizenship and partnership and much else besides are busy transforming the nature of social work. Out of this process of change a new practice is emerging which is clumsily but irrevocably known as *networking*. This book is about networking and is intended to help social workers find their way through unfamiliar territory.

Like many other people, I discovered networking through experience. As a local authority social worker, the idea of networking emerged from linking with and actively promoting links between individuals, groups or organisations for a wide range of purposes associated with my work. I found myself going through this process time and time again. Sometimes, it was a response to the needs of a particular client or service user. At other times, it was focused on broader group or community needs. Sometimes, it was reactive and sometimes it was proactive. However, the issue was always how everyone involved in a particular situation could be helped to work more effectively with one another.

I realised this was something new. Nothing I had read or been taught seemed to adequately describe this process of inter-personal, intergroup and inter-agency work. It wasn't casework; it wasn't community work; and it wasn't group work, although — as if to confuse me further — it sometimes involved aspects of all three. For a time, I thought of it as *community social work* because I knew it was a community practice. But at best, this label seemed to fit only part of what I later came to describe as *networking*.

In retrospect, I was part of a general movement of welfare professionals and service users who were disenchanted with standardised, bureaucratised and institutionalised responses to human need. We were seeking to develop alternatives by breaking down some of the barriers that isolated and oppressed service users and welfare professionals alike. This entailed finding new, more informal and democratic ways of doing things and placing a strong emphasis on communication and cooperation rather than conflict and competition. Networking, is best seen, therefore, as a practice which has grown out of the quest for community partnership.

1

Community partnership

For social workers it is not enough simply to declare that individual 'clients are fellow citizens' (BASW, 1980) and therefore partners. The relationship between social workers and their clients does not exist in a vacuum. It has been argued that the 'ultimate moral basis' of citizenship is the web of reciprocal relationships — the *community* (Jordan, 1990, p. 70). If this is so, then the community is always present in any partnership. For social workers, this is not just an abstract principle. People can only be related to in the context of their communities (Holman, 1983 p. 70) and it is impossible to conceive of social work except in the context of its own 'network of helping agencies and professions' (Payne, 1986a, p. 1).

For social workers and others seeking to put partnership principles into practice, this principle has a number of implications. Firstly, partnership involves working with all those concerned in a particular situation. Secondly, partnerships may serve the interests of more than one person. Even when there is a named client. The process of collaboration is likely to have an impact on all members of the partnership. Thirdly, professionals have to be prepared to share power both with one another and with the communities they serve. Anyone can network. It is something which can be practised by nurses, community workers, health education workers and other professionals, as well as by social workers. Moreover, individuals and groups including service users can network on their own behalf, either with one another or with professionals. For all these reasons, I shall frequently refer to partnership as *community partnership*.

Networking

It is not enough simply to know where we want to go. We have to know how to get there. This is why community partnership as the goal, and networking as the method are 'two sides of the same coin'. And why this book is about networking as a community partnership practice.

It is worth noting that only a few years ago a book on networking would have been inconceivable. Now, however, we have become almost too familiar with this relatively new word. For example, it has been seen as *the* essential ingredient of community care (Laming, 1989, p. 19). When a group of London community workers were asked recently to describe their work, all replied that they were engaged in *networking*[1].

Although, networking emerged unobtrusively, debates about inter-agency collaboration, partnership, empowerment and choice have thrust it into the limelight. Although it has received a lot of attention networking has not been clearly defined. Networking may be 'an idea whose time has come', but there is a real danger of it becoming 'all things to all people' and therefore fashionable but meaningless jargon. To avoid making this mistake, we need to establish a definition of what networking is and how it can help develop community partnership.

At first sight, it seems as if the task of defining networking will be rather like trying to grasp hold of a particularly slippery fish. For example, the term *networking* can be applied to any or all of the following:

> Chairing a conference in which relatives, neighbours, a home help, a district nurse and a GP discuss ways of working together more effectively to help a frail and mentally confused old person;
> Creating a framework of communication and collaboration between a team of health visitors and a team of social workers;
> 'Caring for the carers' of a young man with severe learning difficulties by arranging respite care, home help support, and access to a support group to enable them to continue caring;
> Forging links between a number of local agencies to enable them to support one another;
> A black worker building an authority-wide support network for himself to overcome isolation within a predominantly white section of a local authority;
> Disabled people linking up with one another to campaign for legislative change;
> Putting together a *care package* to enable an old man to continue living in his own home although he can no longer wash or cook for himself.

The list could go on and on. But the task is not as complex as it seems. There is something which all these practices have in common. In every case the focus is on developing 'a specific set of linkages' (Mitchell, 1969, p. 2), in which the *quality of relationships* in the *set* or *network* is in some way related to the *principles of community partnership.*

These principles include both 'choice' (Wagner, 1988) and empowerment. There are relatively few networks to which individuals or groups have to belong (Bott, 1971, p. 222) and yet those who *opt in* to a social network based on community partnership principles gain access to information, emotional and practical support, and in some circumstances, at least an opportunity to define themselves in new and more autonomous ways. These sort of choices are potentially *empowering*, because in a variety of ways they enable individuals and groups to gain control over their environment and help others to do the same.

This gives us a working definition of networking as:

all those activities which enable separate individuals, groups or organisation to join with one another in social networks which enhance communication and/or active cooperation and create new opportunities for choice and empowerment for at least some if not all of those taking part.

Two myths about networking

There are many myths about networking, but we can dispose of two straight away.

One myth is that networking is concerned only with *natural* or pre-existing social networks. But community partnerships may in some circumstances be entirely *artificial* (Garbarino, 1983, p. 5). Networking itself, as a planned and purposeful acitivity, is hardly *natural* and therefore any community partnership which arises as a result of it cannot be *natural* either. Few of the partnership networks described in this book are very *natural*. Most are planned and purposeful.

For example, case management (*see* chapter 6) is concerned with meeting the care needs of a specific individual by linking *informal* and *formal* carers together in thoroughly planned ways to create an effective personal support network. Likewise, networking between social work teams or between disability activists consists of deliberately seeking to develop links between like-minded groups to maximise opportunities for mutual support, practical help, and the planning of collective strategies (*see* chapter 7).

A second myth is that networkers have no interest in individual human beings and have a rather manipulative attitude to them. Networking stresses the need for a unique rather than a standard response to human problems. It holds a belief in the ability of individuals and groups to actively make and remake their social worlds and is very much in tune with the traditional social work values of *acceptance, self-determination* and respect for those we are trying to help. No community partnership can function unless the individuals within it relate to one another as partners. This is as true of inter-agency networks (*see* chapter 4) as of personal support networks (*see* chapters 5 and 6)[2].

Need for good partnership practice

Developments in child care, community care and community health now make networking not just a *good idea* but a *practice necessity*.

Social workers involved in child protection work spend much of their time linking up with other professionals. The success of this work often depends on the quality of these links, as can be seen when something goes wrong, a child dies and the subsequent report finds that poor communication was one of the factors involved.

Social workers involved in community care planning and implementation with nurses and health service administrators need to ensure that the links they create are strong enough to sustain innovative programmes of care and rehabilitation relying on high levels of mutual trust and cooperation.

Those involved in health education work with drug injectors, (eg promoting needle exchanges to prevent the spread of HIV infection) need to establish personal links in clubs, pubs and on the streets with people who may be mistrustful of outsiders (Gaitley and Seed, 1989, pp. 17–27).

If partnership means anything it has to work in stressful and conflict-ridden situations like these, where good intentions are not enough. This book argues that networking can take us beyond good intentions and help us to respond more confidently and creatively to the challenge of making partnership work where it is most needed.

1 Social workers and social networks

Networking on a Friday afternoon

It is Friday afternoon. You are the duty social worker in a busy inner city Social Services Department. Once again Jean Atwood, a single mother has come to the office with her four children, three of whom are under five. As usual, she asks for financial help. She has no money for food and her giro will not arrive until Monday. As usual, you give it. What else can you do? But you realise that giving out money every week is not going to solve this family's problems. The Social Services Department is not an income maintenance agency and you do not have an unlimited hudget. Something else needs to be done, but what?

In situations like this, it is all too easy for social workers to jump to moralistic conclusions and begin to respond in uncaring and unhelpful ways to those who might be seen as *underserving*. But you do not do this. You want to know more about her situation, before you make any decisions.

It does not take you long to discover that Jean Atwood is not a particularly bad manager of her small weekly income, but nevertheless, finds it impossible to make it stretch to the end of the week. Other local families, no better off than her and with budgetary skills no better then hers, nevertheless do not have to make a humiliating trip to the Social Services Department office every week. This is a puzzle that you need to solve. You need to discover what it is about her situation which tilts the balance of her life from just managing to not managing.

When you discover that Jean Atwood has recently left her husband after years of putting up with violent abuse including *marital rape* and that she has been moved to an area where she is not known in order to help her to hide from him because he has threatened to injure her if he finds her, you begin to discover why she cannot live on the money she receives from the Department of Social Security and why finance is just one aspect of the problem situation.

Her flat is damp, poorly insulated and very expensive to heat. She does not know anyone who can advocate on her behalf to the local authority Housing Department. She cannot always take the children with her when she goes out, but she has to pay for any babysitting she uses. The supermarket is two miles away from where she lives.

Buses are few and far between and as she doesn't know the person who organises bulk shopping expeditions on the Estate, she buys all her food from the expensive local *corner shop*. She doesn't know about the *boot sales* and jumble sales which are a source of cheap, good quality clothing and does not know any one who can look out for bargains for her. Many of the local women borrow money from one another or feed one another's children when money is tight. Not knowing, anyone, she cannot do this. In other words, she has no access to the informal social networks which make it possible to survive in the local area. She sees some of her old friends but very infrequently and cannot rely on them for help.

Jean Atwood has no GP, no contact with health visitors, or play-groups and takes no part in activities at the local family centre. She is forced to rely on her own rapidly diminishing mental, emotional, physical and financial resources. But this does not make her inde-pendent. Rather it makes her inappropriately dependent on the Social Services Department of the Local Authority.

Having obtained this sort of information about Jean Atwood, you might be thinking that her financial problems were only one aspect of a more general lack of social support which is also making her anxious and depressed and even less likely to meet people and make new friends. Although her financial problems are real enough, you begin to suspect that her trips to the Social Services Department might also be a more general *cry for help*.

By thinking about Jean Atwood, in this way, you are already adopting a network perspective. If you find ways of linking her to key individuals in her local area, particularly local women with children. If you introduce her to a GP and a health visitor and work with them to advocate for urgent housing repairs on health and social grounds; if you introduce Jean Atwood to the local family centre and if you help her to take an active part in all this, then you are networking.

Networking is an attempt to make use of a general understanding of social network patterns and processes in order to ease the development of community partnerships. In our example, this would involve facilitating the development of community part-nerships between yourself, Jean Atwood, her neighbours, other mothers, health professionals, and family centre workers. In sub-sequent chapters, we will look in some detail at the creation of community partnerships like these. Before we do so, we need to explore the social network basis of community partnership.

Social networks

It has long been argued that social networks can help to solve social problems (eg Maguire, 1983). But it is not always clear what people mean when they say this.

The word *network* can be used as a *metaphor* to refer to any kind of general and unspecified interconnectedness in society (Mitchell, 1969, p. 1). But this can obscure as much as it reveals about social reality, encouraging us to believe in bland and even misguided generalities. Examples are the idea that all networks are somehow *natural* and spontaneous, or that all networks are supportive.

This loose thinking can contribute to a 'rosetinted' view of reality (Bulmer, 1987, pp. 137–138). The reality, as Beresford and Croft demonstrate – in their study of attitudes to community and network in Brighton – is that only some people are involved in actively caring for and supporting others outside their immediate family and that they often do so in very difficult circumstances (Beresford and Croft 1986, p. 78–158). For some the *community* is a real and living thing, but for others it is clearly a myth which has no relevence to their own experience.

> I wouldn't say there is a community spirit (Beresford and Croft, 1986, p. 85)

> Its not friendly. There's funny neighbours...

> People here don't want to know (Beresford and Croft, 1986, p. 94)

Some of those interviewed by Beresford and Croft acknowledged that an informal network of care and support did exist but felt themselves excluded from it.

> I think there is a degree of community, but I don't feel part of it (Beresford and Croft, 1986, p. 86).

For some people this feeling was very acute.

> I've got nothing. I've got no support

But it was not clear that everyone who felt isolated actually wanted more contact with other people.

> I live in my own little world — don't join in

> I keep myself to myself (Beresford and Croft, 1986, pp. 108–109).

These sort of comments indicate that we need a concept of social networks which takes account of the specific ways in which people relate to one another. In other words, we need to think of social networks as 'social fields'.

> I find it convenient to talk of a social field of this kind as a *network*. The image I have is of a set of points some of which are joined by lines. The points of the image are people, or sometimes groups, and the lines indicate which people interact with each other. (Barnes, J. A. 1954 , p. 43).

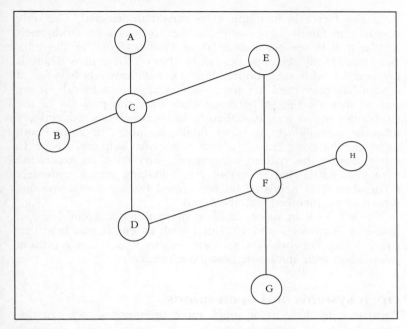

Figure 1

Figure 1 represents a *social field* of this kind. A, B, C, D, E, F, G, and H are individuals or groups interacting in a particular way with one another. C, for example is interacting with A,B,D and E but not with F, G, and H. Moreover A and B are interacting only with C and not with each other. F and C have no contact with each other but both have contact with E and D. This illustrates that individuals and groups participating in a social network do not neccessarily have, and are unlikely to have, contact with all other individuals and groups participating in the same social network. Interestingly, even if we assume that all these relationships are equally supportive, this network is much more supportive of some of its members than others. C, for example receives a lot of support from A, B, D and E, whereas G and H appear to be rather isolated. This kind of information may be quite significant for social workers.

Let us suppose that the social field to which Figure 1 refers is an extended family network and that A, B, C, D, E, F, and G are all separate households and that G is a nuclear family unit — the Godstones — consisting of Mr Godstone, his wife Jean Godstone and their daughter Emma Godstone. There are indications that Emma has been sexually abused by Mr Godstone. If there has been abuse then the relative isolation of the Godstone family may be a key factor in enabling it to remain undetected. The only contact the family have with their relatives is Jean Godstone's regular trips to see her mother Louise Farmer (F on the diagram). But Emma rarely accompanies her mother on these trips. There is no contact with neighbours. Emma's withdrawn behaviour at school has prevented her from making any close friends. If we put all this together it becomes clear how the position of the Godstones within their extended family network has reduced any informal surveillence by other family members to a minimum effectively blocking Emma's access to informal help and advice. In other words, the pattern of network interaction increases the exploitive patriarchal power of Mr G making Emma extremely vulnerable. This needs to be recognised by any social workers who become involved with the family.

We will look in more detail at networking and child sexual abuse in chapters 5 and 10. But I wish to emphasise here that every social network has its own pattern which can represent information with immediate practice relevence[3].

Open systems and open minds

Because it is likely to be much more open-ended, we can distinguish a social network from a social group, where everyone knows everyone else (Benson, 1987, p. 5).

> In network formation... only some, not all of the component individuals have social relationships with one another. In a network, the component external units do not make up a larger social whole: they [the component external units] are not surrounded by a common boundary (Bott, 1957, pp. 58–59).

The social network concept therefore describes a whole range of relatively fluid and informal social phenomena (Srinivas and Beteille, 1964, p. 166). They may be of great significance for those working in a rapidly changing society such as our own in which traditional institutions may no longer provide the frameworks within which people lead their lives. It also opens up the possibility of an alternative to operating through formal structures of power and authority. This is an alternative which we need to be flexible enough to grasp, especially if formal structures are oppressive.

Let us take two examples:

1. Family networks and family work
The continuing movement away from traditional patterns of family life (Robertson Elliot, 1986, pp. 34–72) provides a good example of how network awareness can enhance our understanding of the

contemporary family and result in more supple and sensitive forms of family work.

The concept of the family as an integrated social group may be adequate for work with a relatively isolated nuclear family household. If the parents divorce, remarry and form new *reconstituted* families (Robertson Elliot, 1986, pp. 134–176), the resulting pattern of relationships will be a network rather than a group (Rands, 1988, p. 128). Moreover it may well be a network in which different individuals have very different relationships with one another. For example the children of divorced parents may continue to see both of them, they may cease to have any but the most minimal contact with each other. As a result, children and parents may have very different concepts of what constitutes their family. If there were a social worker or health visitor involved, they would need to recognise that the family — at least as far as the children are concerned — is not a household but rather a network of relationships running across household boundaries. This should also alert them to the possibility of a conflict of interest between parents and children.

Parents may wish to increase their own sense of personal security by minimising their contact with each other using their new family boundaries to exclude each other. They may assume that this is also in the best interests of the children because it will produce more stability. In fact, it is likely to be quite damaging, from the children's point of view as it destroys the family as it exists for them. Knowing this, it should be possible to engage the parents in a discussion about this possible conflict of interest and ways of meeting the needs of the children.

The ideology of the nuclear family is so dominant in our society (Gittins, 1985), that even professional workers may confuse myth and reality. One advantage of the social network approach is in describing families as they are, rather than as we have been taught to see them. Moreover, if social workers are to work in partnership with families, as they are increasingly expected to do (*Children Act*, 1989, s. 22(4)) then the social network approach helps us to see that it must be a partnership which takes account of different interests and relationships.

2. Organisations and organisational networks

Most social work agencies are formal hierarchical structures composed of tightly bounded work groups associated with fixed roles. They are also complex patterns of informal interaction between individuals which may exercise a major influence on the whole *culture* of the agency.

Relationships within a social work team might be good. But this would not preclude women members of that team meeting with other women in the Department for mutual support. This might be even more necessary if within the same office, all influential positions within the union and on working parties were filled by members of a well established informal network or *local mafia* composed of men who used to work together prior to a recent reorganisation. A women's network could help women in the agency by providing information about entitlements of specific relevence to women. Examples might be *dependency leave*, *maternity leave* or career development opportunities, such as new posts, positions on working parties, etc. It could also enable those women who had achieved some prominence within the agency to act as role models or mentors for those who had not yet done so (Nutter, 1991, pp. 18–19).

If you feel oppressed within your agency, an awareness of organisational networks and a willingness to establish supportive and empowering networks with others who share the same oppression is likely to be of direct benefit to you. Through its eventual impact on organisational culture and decision making it is likely to improve the nature of the services which you are able to offer to those who come to you for help because of their own experiences of oppression.

Network membership

There are two ways we can define the membership of a social network.

We can define it by a particular *frame of reference* (Mayer, 1962, p. 275). A community work example may illustrate some of the advantages and disadvantages of this approach.

A community worker has been employed as part of a concerted effort by the Local Authority to *upgrade* the Rivendale Estate Council Estate which has been variously described in the local press as a *Problem Estate*, a *Sink Estate* or even as a *No-Go Area*. It is officially known as a *Neglected Estate*. For the community worker the geographical boundaries of the Estate are an obvious and appropriate *frame of reference* which focuses attention on the lives of Rivendale inhabitants.

The Estate may remain the only *frame of reference* for some time, as the community worker observes the comings and goings of the individuals and groups who live there and builds his own relationship with some of them. However, the community worker may become increasingly aware of certain issues which affect some people more than others: some people on this Estate are more disadvantaged than others. At this stage, the community worker is likely to start thinking in terms of more finely tuned *frames of reference* which relate to *various* minority groups on the Estate. For example the issue of unemployment may have a major impact on the life of the whole Estate, but only 30 per cent of adults are actually unemployed. Using Unemployment as a *frame of reference*, the community worker focuses on the pattern of contact between all those classified as Unemployed on the Estate in order to assess whether or not they had access to mutual support, opportunities for socialising with one another, and working together on *right to work* campaigns.

Whilst useful, this type of *objective* approach can give too much power to professionals, leading to network definitions which may not correspond accurately to the reality of the *subjective network* (Srinivas and Beteille, 1964, p. 166), or the way in which individual's experience their own networks and may indeed seriously distort the nature of this experience. If a *frame of reference* is to be meaningful it has to be based upon discussion and negotiation and never be imposed in a rigid or dogmatic way. For example, Unemployment may seem so closely bound up with issues of Racism for some young Black people that to separate it and give it priority over other issues such as Police Harassment might seem to them a denial of their experiences as Black People. In this context, any community worker who adopted a *colour blind* approach to Unemployment could fairly be accused of racism and would be unlikely to gain the support of the Black Community on Rivendale. One might predict that any initiatives flowing from such a *colour blind* approach would be almost certain to fail or to be seen as for *whites only*.

An alternative more sensitive approach to the way in which people relate but less easy to match with collective needs or issues is to start with a specific individual or group and work outwards. If this is done in relation to a specific individual it is usually referred to as the *personal network* approach (eg Mitchell, 1969).

When interested in the support which is available to particular individuals we invariably focus on the *personal network*. An example is a community care assessment. The health of an elderly person might suddenly deteriorate, leading that person to request additional help from the local authority Social Services Department. If we think of this as a network issue it is clear that a general assessment of the existing level of support in the personal network is needed in order to assess the need for new resources. Social workers would only be able to make this assessment by interviewing both the client and those members of the personal network already actively supporting the elderly person. The best way of supporting the client might be through supporting those members of the personal network acting as carers. But there are other people involved, as well and one of the difficulties with the personal network approach is that it is not obvious how to identify those we need to talk to.

One way forward, is to distinguish between key relationships and those which are less significant, on the basis of how direct or indirect the interactions are (Barnes, 1969, pp. 58–72).

The social worker will need to work closely with the informal carers and consider and consult their families. The latter's attitudes could decisively influence the ability of the carers to continue to function. But it is unclear if anything would be gained by talking to those in contact with the families of the carers if they are not in contact with either the carers or the person for whom they are caring.

This example shows how practice judgements often need to be informed by both *subjective* or person-centred and *objective* or issue-based criteria. But however we do it, an ability to define who is and who is not a significant member of a social network is critical it enables us to know; whom to talk to.

Close-knit and loose-knit networks

Networking enables us to gauge the amount of interdependency or *connectedness* in a social field (Bott, 1971, p. 59).

In a highly interdependent social field there will be few holes in the network *mesh*. (Barnes, 1954, p. 44). On the other hand, where there is little interdependency there will be many holes in the network *mesh*. This makes it possible to distinguish between *close-knit networks* and *loose-knit networks* (Bott, 1971, p. 59).

Figures 2 and 3 illustrate both networks.

Holes in a network *mesh* may be so wide that there is little or no contact between network members. Sometimes this amounts to a pattern of avoidance based on *long-standing grudges* (Broderick, 1988 p. 227). Adolescents described as *out of control* may come from families which have fragmented in this way. Because he or she is the only person in contact with the members of the family network, the adolescent effectively controls family communication which makes it impossible for there to be any coherent family response to his or her difficulties. Power is likely to exacerbate self-destructive behaviour. Thus social workers need to restore contact between the adults to help them to regain the control they need to restore caring.

In some circumstances, network relationships may be very *loose-knit* not because of animosity, but because there has been no contact or communication. Often networks of professionals who may all be involved very intensively with a particular

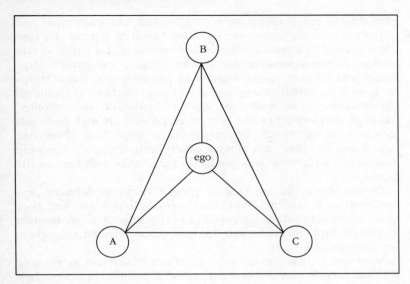

Figure 2

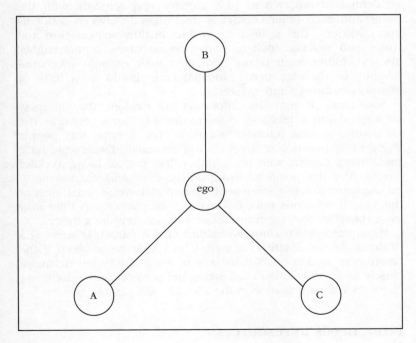

Figure 3

individual or family may have no real contact with each other.

Having recently taken over the supervision of a particular case I was invited to attend a *professionals' meeting* at a family centre to discuss new developments. It was complex involving a large family and an even larger number of professionals. I was struck by how little contact these social workers, teachers, educational psychologists, and residential workers had with one another. Although many of them had been working skilfully with particular members of the family for many years, some had never met before and had little idea of what others were doing. Or if it were compatible with what was going on with other members of the family!

Clients often find the lack of contact between different professionals quite baffling. 'Why don't you talk to one another?' they quite reasonably ask. Consequences of not *talking to one another* vary from duplication of effort, to dramatic and dangerous gaps in service provision.

Moreover only by reviewing the pattern of services as a whole with the service-user can one get any idea of their impact on their life.

Sometimes too much *connectedness* can be a problem. In some residential homes, where staff identify very strongly with the home and each other contact is discouraged between residents and outsiders. This is likely to restrict healthy self-criticism and foster bad practice including in extreme cases, human rights' abuses[4]. Moreover it is not consistent with *normalisation* philosophy or the idea that residential care should be a form of *community care* (Wagner, 1988)

Sometimes it may be important to explore the interplay between different levels of *connectedness* within a network. The community worker referred to earlier, may discover that people living in one particular street on the Rivendale Estate may have much more contact with one another than people living in other streets. Also that residents living on the *close-knit* street seem to be disproportionately influential. They may have secured most of the official positions on the Tenants' Association and they may even speak for the rest of the Estate without consulting them.

Here, the relative *close-knittedness* of this particular street is a problem for the Estate as whole. It can only be resolved if the community worker enables the rest of the estate to interact more closely with one another challenging the position of the dominant clique by full participation in the Tenants' Association.

From needs to resources

The number of *steps* or intermediaries required to get from one part of a network to another (Mitchell, 1969, pp. 12–19) may have important consequences. If too many *steps* are involved it may not be realistic to expect people to find their own way. Unless the steps can be reduced to a manageable number, it may not be possible for people to make contact with the network resources they need. A rough estimate of how many *steps* between a need and a resource is essential if social workers are to make informed judgements about how best to help individuals, families or community groups satisfy needs.

A young father, most of whose friends are male and single might because of death or divorce suddenly become a single parent. Nearby a number of young mothers may have organised a playgroup and a baby sitting circle. But the young man might be prevented from making contact with the baby sitting circle because none of his friends have any direct contact with these young women or even with friends of these young women and taboos on cross gender contact between strangers might make it impossible for him to introduce himself. A social worker or health visitor who had contact both with this young man and the young women in the child care group and who was aware of the problem might be able to act as intermediary, introducing the young man to the group and closing the gap between needs and resources.

Brokers

In any social network there are some people with a particularly wide *range* of personal contacts (Mitchell, 1969, p. 19). Sometimes they effectively control contact between one network and another. If they do so they are network *brokers* (Mayer, 1966, p. 114).

Brokers act as gatekeepers controlling access to a range of network contacts. Access to a network might depend on establishing a relationship with them. A social work team moving into a new patch office in an area traditionally suspicious of the local authority might begin to win acceptance by establising links with key figures who could act as brokers.

Sometimes an awareness of who can act as a broker in a more specific way can be very important.

For example, I was a member of a social work team which wanted to offer advice, information and counselling services to homeless young people living in temporary accommodation in the local area. We realised that these young people were frequently not willing to contact us directly. In the case of the older ones this was based partly on lack of information about the services they might get from a social worker and also on a feeling that social workers would not understand or be sympathetic to their problems. In the case of the younger ones this avoidence of social workers was additionally based on a fear that they might be forcibly sent home or *taken into care* if they asked for help.

Faced with this problem, we decided to make use of our contacts with youth workers in a local *drop-in* centre and staff at a local hostel asking them to disseminate information about services and encourage young people to make direct contact on the understanding that social workers would always seek to work with young people in trouble rather than force them to go home or to come into care, unless there was really no alternative. On the basis of this understanding the youth workers and hostel staff were willing to act as *brokers* mediating between the team and local young people.

An awareness of who the brokers are and how to make contact with them is often of vital significance for anyone trying to establish a service where there is little trust or confidence in *The Welfare*.

Exclusionary networks and networks of empowerment

Analysis of the *composition* (Rands, 1988, p. 129) of a network sometimes reveals that certain categories of people are being excluded from it.

For example, a drop-in centre for unemployed people might decide to advertise itself by informal *word of mouth* which might appear to have worked very well until the organisers realise that there are no Black unemployed people using the centre. Given the high rates of local Black unemployment this can only be explained by the racism of the drop-in centre's informal network.

Similar implicit *exclusionary* devices whether based on race, class or gender are common, particularly in those networks where membership provides access to wealth, power or prestige. One might call such a network an exclusionary network because of its concern with narrowly defined membership criteria. The quintessential example of such an exclusionary network is the so called *Old Boys Network* which operates to ensure that preferment in a whole range of situations goes to White, Male, Upper Class members of the network.

If it is clear that people are being informally but quite systematically excluded from services, it is likely that an exclusionary network is operating. The power of these networks derives from their ability to broker contact between services and the outside world according to their own definition of who should get them. The only way to challenge them is to develop alternative anti-discriminatory forms of brokerage.

Having recognised a racism problem, in addition to challenging White members about it, the drop-in workers in the above example would need to appoint some Black workers if none were present on the staff and actively build links between the Centre and members of the local Black community not only to attract Black members but to build sources of support for these members who might otherwise be vulnerable to the undercurrent of racism which is likely to still permeate the life of the Centre.

Challenging an exclusionary network is best done through the development of an empowering network with its own distinctive characteristics.

If network relationships enable oppressed people to challenge some aspects of their oppression these relationships can be seen as a *network of empowerment*. Empowering networks may like exclusionary networks be for certain sorts of people only. But there the similarity ends. A women's support network may exclude men in order to *raise consciousness* and encourage assertiveness among its members. The exclusion of men is not an attempt to maintain privilege but in contrast, an attempt to facilitate the kind of personal development which could lead to a challenge to the exclusionary practices associated with the Old Boys Network among others.

Developing a network of empowerment may require professional workers to confront not only their own attitudes to issues like race, gender, sexuality, age and disability but also their assumptions about professional power. This may be painful. But if we are serious about partnership and empowerment we ourselves need to share power (Adams,1990, pp. 132–33).

A word of warning. Even amongst the relatively powerless some may be more powerful than others. A danger confronting empowering networks is that energy which should be used challenging oppression can be used to maintain the position of a small clique. Where an ostensibly empowering network becomes dominated by a clique it may resemble an exclusionary network and oppress those on whose behalf it may claim to speak. Professionals hoping to facilitate the development of empowering networks need to be aware of these issues because an empowering network should empower everyone.

Reciprocity

A network is an exchange system and it has been suggested that *mutual exchanges* lie at the very heart of a healthy social network (Garbarino, 1986, p. 35). There are many examples of networks which appear to function on the basis of reciprocity, eg friendship networks. However many networks are characterised by various degrees of *directness* or relative lack of reciprocity (Mitchell, 1969, pp. 24–26). Complete reciprocity may not always be desirable if it prevents some people taking an initiative on behalf of others. For example the presence of *natural neighbours* or *help-givers* on whom others are dependent, appears to be crucial to the development of some neighbourhood networks (Collins, & Pancoast, 1976, p. 21).

But although *directness* may be useful in the short-term, in the long-term it can lead to instability. *Natural neighbours* may fall ill or move away, perhaps to escape the stress of taking on too much responsibility. Total reciprocity may not be realistic for example where dependent people are being cared for intensively by family, friends, or neighbours. Opportunities for carers to meet and support one another (Trevillion, 1988, pp. 302–307) should be explored as ways of strengthening informal caring networks. Some element of reciprocity is essential to any partnership.

In practice, it is very difficult to objectively evaluate the level of reciprocity in an exchange. In most cases allowing the members of the network to evaluate their own exchanges is likely to be more effective. When people do this, they are likely to take all aspects of their interactions into account and not just the more tangible ones. Therefore, issues such as the extent to which all views are listened to; that everyone shares equally in decision making may be as important as everyone's contributing equal amounts of time or practical assistance in determining whether people feel that they are in a geniune partnership with one another. Reciprocity may turn out to be inseparable from democracy!

Summary

Community partnership involves working with social networks. Working with social networks involves working with open-ended *social fields* rather formally constituted social groups or formal organisational structures of a bureaucratic nature. Insofar as both groups and organisations can be oppressive networking opens up new possibilities of empowerment.

A rigid formula cannot define who should be partners because social networks and therefore partnerships are situational. Partnerships need to reflect a particular *frame of reference*, ie a particular issue, need, purpose, or problem, and the pattern of interaction.

They need to take account of the way individuals or groups may perceive situations and their relationships with others.

Partners can be very intensively involved with one another or loosely associated with one another, ie partnerships can be either relatively close-knit or relatively loose-knit. Networking is concerned with facilitating the development of patterns of interaction or linkage appropriate to particular types of partnership. In this process, a number of issues need to be borne in mind.

1. The ease with which network partners can gain access to one another has implications for individuals or groups seeking to gain access to network resources.
2. Network brokers occupy pivotal positions in any community partnership and the relationship cultivated with them may make the difference between the success or failure of the partnership.
3. Some networks are oppressive, others are empowering and community partnerships can help to empower individuals and groups by helping them to come together in their own networks to support one another and confront their oppression in collective ways.
4. Social networks are exchange systems and although some people may need to take the lead from time to time, on the whole, it is probably better to encourage interdependency rather than dependency.

2 Community partnership: practices and processes

Networking: an enabling strategy

In the last chapter we looked at how an understanding of social networks could help social workers, community workers and others to work more effectively in a wide range of situations. But networking is more than just a matter of knowing about social networks or even knowing how to intervene in them for particular purposes. Networking consists of applying this knowledge to a specific goal: the development of community partnerships. This chapter will look at how this can be done.

Whilst we can define partnership in a number of different ways, few would disagree that it involves sharing. It is hard to see how any relationship which did not provide opportunities for sharing information, consultation, mutual support and empowerment could qualify as a partnership[5]. But knowing this is not enough. We need to know how to practice partnership and enable sharing to take place. I will argue that networking's contribution to community partnership is that it enables individuals, groups or organisations to develop relationships with one another that make sharing possible. But this involves facilitating a number of very specific although interdependent processes.

1. Enabling interpersonal relationships

Caring

Whenever we talk about social networks, we are talking about the way in which people relate to and interact with one another. Social networks are the *personal order of society* (Mitchell, 1969, p. 10). We cannot afford to ignore this (Bennett, 1980) even when we are focusing on inter-agency networks because it is not agencies which interact with one another, but people representing them.

22

Partnership involves respect for other people and caring about their physical, mental and emotional well being. We need to show that we care and that we are not simply exploiting their willingness to help. In the past, welfare agencies have often failed to do this, for example, by leaving carers to cope on their own, whilst hiding behind the rhetoric of community care.

> When Mum left the hospital, after the stroke we saw no one. No one said, 'Look, you're going to have to watch your back with the lifting'. I put on three stone in weight, I was so depressed. You almost need something like a teacher training course before you bring them home. It's not fair to anyone. We didn't have the commode, we didn't know about the inco (incontinence) service. I didn't know who to turn to: I was given no telephone numbers. She didn't have a telephone for a year. I said she must have a telephone. But they said there were two people in the house. I said my mother can't move, Dad had to keep coming round in the cold to get me, what if he's ill? It was the same when I asked for Meals on Wheels. Mum had just had the stroke and I was still working. She (someone from the Social Services) came and looked at me and said, 'Can't you do it?' She wouldn't let me have it (Hicks, 1988, p. 9).

But exploitation is not always as obvious as this. Sometimes it can take the form of simply allowing people to carry too much responsibility. We may need to stop people exploiting themselves. *Members of disadvantaged communities* may sometimes, at considerable personal cost, take on too much responsibility for the maintenance of community groups. If they fall ill or for some other reason cannot carry on supporting everyone else, these community groups may collapse or at the very least become temporarily ineffective because no one else is able to take their place. (Taylor, 1983, p. 27).

Trust

In a partnership people need to trust one another. Networking is about enabling this to happen. But if we want to develop trust, we first have to show that we ourselves can be trusted.

Sometimes people will test you out by giving you a task which may not be achievable but will demonstrate whether or not you are genuinely committed to their interests. If you are given one of these impossible tasks it may be worth consoling yourself with the thought that what is at issue is not your success or failure but rather your commitment. If you demonstrate commitment that may be all anyone expects.

This happened several times when I worked in a

neighbourhood office, often in the early stages of making contact with groups of people who had little reason to trust the State or any of its representatives. In particular, ethnic minority communities who might have experienced persecution and exploitation in their countries of origin and then individual and institutional racism in the UK often began to relate to our neighbourhood team in this way.

> On one occasion the task we were set involved trying to help a person who had a number of obsessions about cooking and cleanliness. Working with him was exhausting and not especially productive, but I stuck with it for some time before I was forced to admit that there was little I could do to help. Although I felt rather negative about the whole experience, I soon realised that other members of this man's community were beginning to make contact with us as a result of seeing that we could be trusted to respond positively to requests for help.

Another aspect of the interpersonal dimension of partnership which networkers need to be aware of is the influence social network relationships can have on the way people feel about themselves.

Self-images and images of others
In the case of family networks, many of us would agree with the comment that 'part of one's own self may be put into relatives unconsciously' (Bott, 1971, p. 159). What is perhaps less clear, is that changes in the pattern of network relationships can affect the feelings we have about ourselves. The development of a partnership *set* involves working with both the feelings people have about one another and the feelings they have about themselves.

> A daughter may feel very angry with the mother for whom she gave up her career to care full-time, because she never receives any word of thanks. Her disabled elderly mother may withold gratitude as a way of regaining some control over her daughter who now seems so powerful. Both mother and daughter may project feelings of frustration onto each other and simultaneously introject feelings of worthlessness and powerlessness from each other. Other relatives may visit but very infrequently. Inevitably, but unrealistically, mother and daughter look to each other to meet all their needs and end up punishing and perhaps even abusing each other.

A social worker, called in to help should see two significant features of the mother/daughter relationship. Firstly, that it was unbalanced. The exchanges between mother and daughter were too *directed* and there was little sense of reciprocity. Secondly, the mother/daughter relationship seemed to exist within a *hole* in the family and neighbourhood network, relatively isolated from contact with other people and forcing both mother and daughter to turn in upon themselves and their relationship with each other.

Greater reciprocity could be introduced into the mother-daughter relationship by enabling the mother to do more for herself and finding ways in which the mother could be helpful to her daughter, eg by offering her advice based on life experience. This would reduce the *directedness* or dependency which seems to be generating so much bitterness. It would also challenge the ageism so often linked to the sexism in claustrophobic caring relationships like this.

Involving other members of the family or neighbours as additional *informal* carers and introducing a home help would help to reduce the exclusive dependency of mother on daughter. Ensuring that some male relatives or neighbours were included among the new carers would help to promote the idea that caring can be shared between men and women reducing the intensity of the daughter's feelings of obligation towards her mother.

Helping to create a link between the mother and others of her own age in a nearby day centre or club might give her an opportunity to reminisce, reassuring her about the value of her own life. This would enhance her self-esteem and willingness to do things for herself, in turn reducing her dependency on her daughter. Simply seeing less of her daughter might lead to a more relaxed relationship with her.

For her part the daughter would as a result of the involvement of other people with her mother be able to create new links for herself. She would have more free time to pursue her own social life and might even be able to return to work. This would be likely to improve her self-esteem, making her less vulnerable to negative comments her mother might make about her.

Enabling the daughter to join a carers' group might help her to share her feelings with other people in the same position. Consequent involvement in campaigns on behalf of carers might also help her to value what she was doing.

Networking is relationship work. It is about promoting care; concern and respect; trust and the kind of interactions which help people to feel better about themselves and more positive about one another. All are essential in any community partnership.

2. Enabling community
In the broadest sense, all the processes described in this chapter are community processes. But there are some specific factors to

be considered in relation to communality, ie *'fraternity and cooperation'* (Plant, 1974, p. 17). A key factor in the development of partnership is helping people to develop more fraternal and cooperative relationships with one another.

Communal identity

Many social networks have community potential even if they do not always seem to be based on *fraternity and cooperation*. They provide an opportunity for people to bring *themselves*, in the *totality of their social roles* (Plant, 1974, p. 16) to the making of relationships. It follows from this, that at its simplest level networking can consist simply of giving people the chance to interact with one another as people.

Communality or communal identity is associated with empowerment. Many people who have felt alone with their feelings and problems have found that a collective experience not only overcomes isolation but *offers an escape route from stigmatising labels* (Lindenfield and Adams, 1984, pp. 11–12).

Many disabled people are systematically excluded from so called *public transport* by the fact that the design of buses, tubes and trains takes little account of their needs. It may be very difficult for them to make contact with one another without mediation controlled by an able bodied person driving a car, pushing a wheelchair, organising an *outing*, running a day centre. But without direct and unmediated contact, disabled people may be unable to share their experiences with one another and to explore their common identity as disabled people (Oliver, 1990). If able-bodied people want to enter into a genuine partnership with disabled people, they can do so by helping with transport and other mobility issues but in ways which disabled people control: decisions about how, where, when and for what purposes they meet should be made by disabled rather than able-bodied people. This means that able-bodied helpers need to ensure that their assistance is facilitative rather than intrusive.

If people are forced to interact in ways which reinforce their sense of powerlessness, they will not develop a communal identity. To experience oneself as a disabled person among other disabled people may be empowering but not if the context is an event run by the able-bodied for *the handicapped*!

But even when people are free to interact with one another in the way they want, at first they may not feel particularly close to one another. For example, caring is such a highly privatised experience, that when carers are introduced to one another they may initially feel that they have little in common. It may be necessary to work with feelings of suspicion, mistrust, even competitiveness over a considerable period of time, in order to establish a sense of communal identity.

Enabling choice

Enabling people to feel involved in choices about their own care is a key social work task (Wagner, 1988). Social networks are useful contexts for choice. In any network it is difficult for hierarchies of control to emerge. People on the whole choose whom they want to relate to and even to some extent how they want to relate to them — even within family networks (Bott, 1971, p. 222). But simply leaving service users to make their own decisions unaided is not a viable approach unless people already have access to all the information they need and have developed a high level of self-confidence. If this is not the case then simply putting people in touch with one another and asking them to let you know what they have decided is irresponsible. It is not the absence of *disabling professionals* which in itself generates *enabling and empowerment* (Hadley, Cooper, et al 1987, p. 10). Rather it is the positive experience of being involved. This is more than just having one's say: it is feeling that what one has said makes a difference.

Sometimes democracy will assert itself whatever professionals do or say. For example, a social worker might seek to organise a number of carers to make their caring more *efficient*. In the process, he or she might ask them to do a number of inappropriate things. If one of the carers challenges the control culture by questioning the *wisdom* of the social worker and suggests an alternative plan, the network as a whole, may then support this plan and move to take control.

But it is surely better to work with this process rather than to submit ungraciously to it!

Quality Assurance Groups have been set up in the London Borough of Hammersmith and Fulham to enable people living with HIV to participate in service development. They have shown how people can be involved not only in choices about their own care but in decisions about the way in which HIV services as a whole will evolve. This helps to promote a sense of partnership.

'At the meeting you're putting something back into the community' says Alan, whose initial doubts were quickly dispelled.
'We're all living in the local community,' adds Derek.
'There's a tremendous amount of resources in the community that social services could make use of so the good thing about quality assurance is that we can make some purposeful input.'
(*Social Work Today*, '17.10.91, p. 18)

Enabling choice is about providing positive opportunities for

empowerment. The Hammersmith and Fulham model of Quality
Assurance Groups is one example of providing such an opportunity by linking service user representatives and professionals
together in a working partnership.

Enabling mutual support

Mutual aid or mutual support lies at the heart of the community
process (Hadley, Cooper, et al 1987, p. 11). In any community
partnership members need to be able to turn to one another for
help and support. When it is present we tend to take peer support for granted. But it only really flourishes when a social
network possesses some degree of *connectedness* or interdependency.

Professionals as well as service users can find themselves to be
relatively unsupported.

A number of workers may be involved in providing services for
single homeless people in one inner city area. They may include
four day centre workers employed by two separate voluntary
organisations; a specialist social worker based in a Social Services
Department office preoccupied with child care issues; a detached
youth worker with a particular interest in homelessness; and a
probation officer concerned with the welfare of ex-prisoners. These
workers either feel isolated because their organisations are small or
because their concerns seem to be of little interest to anyone else in
their organisations. To overcome their isolation and/or marginal-
isation they explore ways of connecting with one another. Some of
them meet up for *trouble sharing* once a month at a day centre.
Some exchange telephone numbers and ring one another for advice,
information or practical help on a range of issues from social
security problems to coping with problems such as handling
violence; people drinking on day centre premises; or how a particular borough interprets its responsibilities to homeless people. In
this way they begin to feel that they have a support network which
may prepare the ground for some joint work later on.

In this example, the workers develop their own mutual support
network. But service users or carers are not always able to do this
on their own, partly because they may not have had any
experience of mutual support which might lead them to believe
that such a thing would be possible. In situations like this social
workers and others can help by making use of any opportunities
which present themselves to enable people to begin to interact
with one another and discover that they can be supportive of one
another. For example a series of case conferences or a consultation exercise may be used to facilitate *connectedness* between
carers (Trevillion, 1988).

Overall, enabling community involves enabling people to feel a part of something positive and empowering with which they can identify; through which they feel they can enhance their own choices and the choices available to others; and by which they can feel supported or offer support to others.

3. Enabling, flexibility, and informality

Joint work and the collective ownership of tasks

Conventionally, networks have been classified as belonging to either *informal* or *formal* types (Barclay, 1982, p. xiii) with the possibility of a third mixed or *interwoven* type combining lay and professional care (Bayley, 1978, p. 31). But all community partnerships need to be informal even if they only involve other agencies or other professionals. To make this clear, all the examples illustrating this process of enabling flexibility and informality will be drawn from so called *formal networks*.

Even in a *formal* community partnership, roles need to be constantly renegotiated with a willingness to do this. We can help to promote informality by our own attitudes. For example, we can be responsive to opportunities for joint work with other agencies and other professionals which might be quite innovative.

In one case, involving two children at risk of sexual abuse, I undertook several joint visits with a female probation officer to help the parents talk through their relationship with one another and whether they wanted it to continue — an informal conciliation service. My own child protection responsibilities and the probation officer's befriending and after-care responsibilities overlapped in the area of marital counselling.

This example also highlights another aspect of informality — the informality of network problem solving. Institutionalised and routinised responses to client need, in which every agency focuses on its own conception of its responsibilities allow certain unpopular tasks to be avoided by assuming that someone else will do them. As soon as professionals start relating to each other across institutional boundaries it becomes much more difficult to avoid shared responsibility and professional roles have to be thoroughly refashioned for the task. For this to happen, we may need to actively promote a partnership identity and a sense of collective responsibility. It may only happen if the partnership has experience of working together. By seizing opportunities for collaborative work we put ourselves and others in the position of having to negotiate our roles in the context of a particular piece of work. In doing so, we set ourselves the kind of challenge which is likely to stimulate creativity in ourselves and in our partners.

Overcoming mutual suspicion

The conditions for partnership may depend very heavily on whether people feel able to work informally with one another. Personality factors are relevant and it would be dishonest to pretend otherwise. Nevertheless, people and agencies also need to have the opportunity of getting to know one another if they are to work well together. An informal pattern of contact is often best suited to encourage informal styles of collaborative work.

In one child protection situation, I found that it was possible to establish a particularly good understanding with a health visitor and a schoolteacher. Prior to this case my team had developed some informal contacts with the clinic and the school devoted to finding out more about one another. I think it certainly helped to cooperate with one another in the stressful circumstances of child protection which otherwise might have led all of us to adopt defensive and negative attitudes. As a result we were able to undertake quite ambitious, collaborative, interdisciplinary work with one another.

Sometimes, it may be necessary to spend time dismantling negative stereotypes about one another before starting any work.

Within Social Services Departments, relationships between social workers and home helps are often very poor and any network involving both social workers and home helps needs to spend time dismantling mutual stereotypes. On one occasion as a social worker I met with group of home helps to discuss future patterns of collaboration. The level of distrust and suspicion in the room was so palpable that I became convinced that social workers and home helps would need to get to know each other before we could hope to work effectively together.

Some time later, however, it became clear to me that working closely alongside one another had transformed relationships. Social workers and home helps in the network had developed personal loyalties which set them somewhat apart from other social workers and home helps who had not shared in this experience of working closely together. However it was also clear that new more flexible and less professionally defensive styles of work were much more easily accepted within the network than outside it where mutual stereotyping continued to thrive.

Networking can build on and develop the potential for informality implicit in any social network. Innovative collaborations;

adaptation of role to task rather than the opposite; collective ownership of decision making; and the development of a more open and tolerant culture within a network through personal trust and respect are all aspects of the *informality* associated with and promoted by networking.

4. Enabling communication

Communication networks

The pattern of partnership in a network will only be as good as the pattern of communication. It is the *communication network* which conveys requests for help and offers of help from *person to person* (Srinivas and Beteille, 1964, p. 168).

Partnership involves access to information and a *communication network* can be seen as a tool for ensuring access to information. Such a network can be seen as a pattern of relationships able to unblock communication by enabling messages to be transmitted along it. Seen in this way a communication network can translate an abstract right to information into something real and practically useful. In the UK for example, the *1989 Children Act* makes it obligatory for social workers to provide more information than ever before to children and families. But such is the complexity of some of this information that it is only likely to be effectively transmitted if all those concerned with caring for children cooperate with one another to create the kind of atmosphere in which people are able to listen to one another. Only when such an atmosphere is created we can say that a real communication network exists.

From time to time, it may be necessary to vary patterns of communication. It is important to recognise that even small changes may well change the basis of the network partnership. For example it may be necessary to send information about a young mother living in a damp flat with her baby to a health visitor and a housing officer. By introducing new professionals there may be anxiety about confidentiality. It will need careful handling and close consultation with the young mother to avoid a crisis in network relationships.

Closed circuits and open circuits

Communication networks exist along a continuum from *closed circuits* to *open circuits* (Srinivas and Beteille, 1964, p. 167). All patterns of network communication have advantages and disadvantages. In encouraging certain patterns of communication to evolve, networkers always need to bear in mind the purpose of the partnership.

Closed circuit partnerships are able to transmit information to every part of the network speedily. The high level of *connectedness* ensures that individuals probably hear the message from several different people simultaneously. At the same time the wide range of transmitters should act as a self correcting device ensuring a minimum of distortion in the message. If distortions do occur, then it may be relatively easy to *broadcast* new correct versions of the message. If we return to the example of a communication network focused on a child *in need*, it is likely that a *close-knit* closed circuit of communication would best serve the interests of the child and those of the partnership, as a whole. In practice this means regular meetings and close contact between a relatively small number of people. This would enable the social worker to ensure that parents or others do not miss out on key bits of information.

A closed circuit of communication may also be a very helpful way of establishing a shared awareness of neighbourhood issues. This is not only relevant for social workers or community workers. It has, for example been suggested that health visitors wanting to know what is going on in their local areas should speak to as many people as possible by *dropping in* on other agencies, attending community forums, inviting people for lunch, etc. (Drennan, 1988, pp. 114–17).

Where confidentiality is an issue, eg when a person has an HIV diagnosis, or where someone has disclosed a history of sexual abuse, then communication should be organised on closed circuit principles. This gives network partners much more control of information. Firstly, it enables them to make clear decisions as to whether or not to pass on confidential information to outsiders. Secondly, if they do decide to do this with the explicit permission of those most involved, then they are able to make access to information conditional upon entering into an expanded network partnership involving responsibilities to the network, as a whole.

Messages passed through an open circuit are likely to be broadcast more quickly and widely than messages passed through a closed circuit. Thus open circuits are more appropriate to spreading a message to as many people as possible. An example of networking to create such an open circuit of communication is by those working in community health education (Gaitley and Seed, 1989, pp. 19–27). Rather than focusing on developing a tightly interwoven partnership, community health educators try to forge links with a wide range of individuals and groups who act as brokers for an even wider range of people. Not only is the health message transmitted widely, it is also varied to suit the needs of different networks.

Community workers have sought to disseminate information by

direct *street* contact with drug users in the hope that at least some of them in turn will pass on advice to other drug users. Efforts have also been made in both Glasgow and London to reach resistant heterosexual networks by making information available at football matches so that the staff and supporters networks may act as a transmission system for health advice.

One feature of all these community health education strategies is that they attempt to use informal networks as channels of communication. Some seek to substitute direct, personal forms of communication for the advertising campaigns which often seem to create more problems than they solve (Wiseman, 1989, pp. 211–12). A fully networked approach to health education would try to move beyond methods of transmitting information to the public and seek to create a dialogue between them and the various *experts*.

> Health educators and health promoters must listen and learn from their prospective clients before they can help them to make more rational decisions about their lives. Liaison, networking, learning and adaptation will be crucial factors in the process of promoting active participation (Wiseman, 1989, p. 219).

Newsletters

Sometimes, network relationships are too *loose-knit* to function unaided as communication networks. Newsletters can help to overcome this problem.

To heighten awareness about HIV infection newsletters containing health advice in the form of cartoons have been produced by the Roadrunners Project and distributed through a variety of agencies and contact points (Gaitley and Seed, 1989, pp. 19–27).

In situations like this a newsletter can not only help to establish communication but may also begin to facilitate the development of closer relationships by advertising meetings, social events, etc.

Transmitting messages

The structure of networks influences the ease of communication, as does the identity of the *transmitter* — the point at which the message enters the *communication network*. If a message enters the network through an individual who is relatively peripheral having only a few links with other members of the network, it may take a long time for the message to circulate. It might even get lost altogether. If on the other hand a message enters the network through a *well connected* individual perhaps a *central figure* of the network (Collins & Pancoast 1976, p. 21), the message may circulate quickly.

In an effort to respond to a request for a mutual support group emanating as I thought, from all those involved in visiting elderly people on a local council estate, I once called a meeting of these *good neighbours*. I assumed that the best person to spread the word about this was the Chair of the Tenants' Association (TA) whom I knew visited some elderly people herself. I could not have been more mistaken. On the day of the meeting, very few people were present. It turned out that the TA Chair in fact knew only one other *good neighbour* and was not the best person to ask. After the meeting I discovered that one of the department's own home helps who lived locally knew most of those involved in the visiting scheme. When she was asked to encourage people to come to the next meeting, most of them turned up. This illustrates the importance of *broadcasting* a message from the most effective place in a network.

Because of their branching structure networks tend to spread rather than target information. Nevertheless, provided the number of intermediaries is kept to a minimum, messages can be targeted through a network to particular individuals.

If a social worker needs to speak to the mother of a child in care who has been avoiding contact with both the social worker and the child, the social worker might try to convey the need for a meeting through an intermediary, eg the child's grandmother.

Although the message might get distorted or never be passed on, there are times when such risks have to be taken because there is no alternative. Using network relationships to target information is however a last resort and always requires the development of a partnership relationship with the person who is brokering or acting as a *go-between*.

Gossip

Communication networks are rarely homogeneous. There are always features which differentiate one bit of the network from another. For example, whether or not one has access to gossip may indicate whether one is a network insider or a network outsider (Epstein, 1969, pp. 121–25).

Although a social network may disseminate relatively neutral information quite widely, the really important information may only circulate within a small *inner circle*. This often seems to happen in those *interwoven* networks of social care in which professionals, volunteers, relatives and others try to collaborate with one another to help a particular individual. Whether the client is a frail elderly person or a young man with a schizophrenic diagnosis the same tendency can be observed. Professionals tend to *gossip* with one another. Moreover in private discussion this *inner circle* may develop a professional consensus — a set of private understandings from which clients, carers, and others are excluded. Wherever these tendencies emerge they have to be challenged by networkers if the partnership, as a whole, is to be empowered.

A community partnership is often only as effective as its communication network. There is no single ideal pattern of communication. Both *open circuits* and *closed circuits* have their place. It is important that we are able to facilitate the pattern of communication that is most appropriate for a particular community partnership and that we ourselves understand how to link up with and communicate along existing channels.

5. Enabling action-sets

Building an action-set
An ability to do things together is inseparable from the partnership concept. In a community partnership this can either mean mobilising support for an individual or action on behalf of a group. Part of a social network which is mobilised for specific purposes is an *action-set* (Mayer, 1966). For social workers the task of action-set mobilisation is a very important aspect of building a network partnership.

Mobilising *responses to adversity* (Barclay, 1982, p. xiii) cannot always be left to that nebulous creature *the community*. Sometimes it involves social workers acting as service brokers. Enabling someone to continue to live in their own home in spite of increasing frailty and a general decrease in mobility, often involves introducing new helpers, both lay and professional into the existing helping matrix. This may solve part of the problem by ensuring that there are sufficient resources available but it still does not mean that these resources will be used effectively. Ways of helping those involved to actively work together need to be found. This is referred to as *interweaving* (Bayley, 1978, p. 31).

Action-sets of all kinds need to be coordinated whether composed of professionals, volunteers or service users. Co-ordination is the key to case management. It is also a vital ingredient of community action; the formation of self-advocacy networks; or cooperation between agencies in order to help *children in need*. As such it has to be a part of any action-set strategy.

Creating action-set potential

Mobilisation around an issue is not always spontaneous. Ironically, those people who may have the smallest and least effective networks may also be of only marginal concern to official welfare agencies. Homelessness is a good example. Both local and national government admit the problem is a serious one and yet because there is no real *ownership* of it, very little seems to be done. Homeless people are always somebody else's problem (Murie, 1988, p. 270). It may be impossible to mobilise action until there is a real concern about the issue among individuals, groups, and agencies whether at a local or national level. But this can be done without bypassing homeless people themselves.

Places for homeless young people to meet and get advice create opportunities to encourage the growth of self-help networks. They also provide opportunities to enable members of networks to share their experiences and put their case to local politicians, housing officers, the media and others.

Networkers have to be concerned with the whole process of action-set mobilisation. For social workers this may involve actively brokering a *care package* or it may mean simply helping potential activists to get in touch and stay in touch with one another, so that they are in a position to work together when the need arises.

Summary

Networking is concerned with enabling partnership. This means enabling five interdependent partnership processes to develop simultaneously.

1. Enabling interpersonal relationships involves an awareness of individuals, their needs and their significance in the overall pattern of network relationships. This includes self-awareness and understanding the fundamental importance of trust in the creation of any partnership.
2. Enabling community involves actively promoting:
   (a) Patterns of interaction which promote a sense of collective identity;
   (b) Freedom of choice and shared decision making; and
   (c) Mutual support.
3. Enabling flexibility and informality involves a willingness to constantly renegotiate roles to work successfully alongside a wide range of other people. It involves sharing responsibility rather than blaming other people if things go wrong.

4. Enabling communication involves ensuring that all network members have access to relevant information. This is not just transmitting information oneself. It involves facilitating the development of a pattern of communication to ensure that all network members can communicate with one another about the issues with which they are concerned. This will depend on the situation. No single pattern of communication will suit all eventualities. Judgement is needed to select appropriate individuals to transmit information.

5. Enabling action-sets involves helping to mobilise an *action-set* to support a member of the partnership; or to take collective action in pursuit of shared goals or interests. Networkers can help people to develop an action-set potential and having done so, assist them to coordinate their actions effectively.

All these processes will be explored in more detail as we look at the way they are combined with one another in various types of community partnership. We will begin with neighbourhood networking the attempt to build localised community partnerships.

3 Patch social work: networking the neighbourhood

Neighbourhoods and neighbourhood partnerships

There is no satisfactory definition of neighbourhood (Williams, 1985, pp. 29–49). Indeed there is a heated debate as to what it really means (Abrams, 1980 p. 18). The idea of neighbourhood has sometimes been expressed in the language of community (Bayley, 1973, p. 12); sometimes in the language of radical left wing politics (O Malley 1977, pp. 54–67). But however it is defined it contains the idea that *face to face* communication can reveal common interests or loyalties which open up the possibility of cooperation and collaboration at a local level.

Patch social work inherits some key practice principles from other forms of neighbourhood work. The concept of the neighbourhood as an informal, flexible and durable resource system comes from the community development tradition (eg Milson, 1974, p. 26). The concept of the neighbourhood as a self-help network comes from the neighbourhood care movement.

> Neighbourhood care is that part of the spectrum of community care that is associated with highly localised schemes, organisations, groups or projects which use local people to provide help or support for other people living near them (Abrams, et al 1989, p. 1).

The history of neighbourhood care shows that it is not always easy to translate the rhetoric of neighbourhoodism into reality. It also shows that localised community partnerships are sometimes possible.

Research on neighbourhood care suggests that some schemes seem to have little orientation to the neighbourhood. Traditional volunteerism may masquerade as neighbourhoodism whilst formalised referral systems, centralised organisational structures and a tendency for *good neighbours* to have little contact with one another (Abrams, et al 1989, p. 80) leads to an emphasis on *care acts* rather than caring relationships (Hedley, 1984).

38

Moreover some schemes exclude precisely those people who may be in most need of a *good neighbour* by ignoring the needs of local working class people (Abrams et al 1989, p. 120). Where this happens the neighbourhood is defined in such a way that it becomes the exclusive preserve of the middle classes (Abrams et al 1989, p. 120).

But there are some neighbourhood care schemes which seem to achieve their aims such as People in Networks (PIN).

People In Networks is here:
● to enable people to help each other when in trouble,
● to get people to know each other to reduce isolation.
(Quoted in Hedley, 1985)

PIN achieves high levels of participation by its members in running its affairs, probably enhanced by the possibility of informal socialising in the shop and office and the fact that the work is shared out evenly, avoiding reliance on a small group of people who could exercise undue influence. (Hedley, 1985, pp. 6–17). It also destigmatises help by enabling those who receive it to join the help giving network at a later date. In this way relatively isolated people are drawn into the central neighbourhood mesh as full participating members.

The success of this scheme and others like it shows that the neighbourhood principle which is at the heart of patch social work can help to draw people together in working partnerships.

Patch social work: interweaving social services and self-help at a local level

If neighbourhoodism in its pure form turns its back on the *welfare environment*, ie the 'established pattern of formally organised services' (Abrams et al, 1989, p. 140) in its attempt to re-energise the purely informal resources of the neighbourhood, patch is, in essence, an attempt to create a new partnership between the *welfare environment* and local people. As such it operates with a very different concept of neighbourhood partnership based on the Seebohm principle of *interweaving* social services and mutual aid/self-help (1968, paras 330–343, 492) but with a specifically *neighbourhood orientation*. This springs from a belief in

> the over-riding importance of locally based informal relationships in providing care for most dependent people and the significance of locally oriented social services in strengthening and reinforcing such networks when they need support (Barclay, 1982, p. 220).

Patch

Going local involves much more than simply building a local office (Hadley and Mcgrath, 1980, p. 97). Social Services offices often seem a *place apart* from the rest of society, inheriting the stigma of the Victorian Poor Law and, entered into only as a last resort. This can be only partly changed by ensuring that the office is open and welcoming in its style, or by encouraging local people to use the office for community group meetings (Hadley and McGrath, 1980, pp. 63–70). The most important element is the development of a 'lively partnership of the statutory, voluntary and informal sections of communities' (Cooper, 1980, p. 30). This entails that professional workers 'engage the community in a dialogue' (Cooper, 1980, p. 30) or to be more precise a whole series of overlapping dialogues.

Patch partnership

Enabling interpersonal relationships

Through its neighbourhood focus, patch has sought to reassert the importance of small scale and more personal forms of caring. For example, one group of patch workers through their local knowledge and local contacts were able to respond to the needs of a number of severely disabled elderly people who had few social contacts. Unable to take advantage of existing social clubs on the patch because of their mobility problems and care needs, they responded positively to a club which met regularly but which also enabled its members to maintain telephone contact with one another if they were too ill to attend. Here a partnership was established between the service users themselves, as well as between service-users, local volunteers and social workers. It worked because it was understood that all those involved were genuinely committed to one another and responsive to each others' needs.

Helping local carers to link up with one another by helping them to meet with and mutually support one another either in a group or through a more flexible carers network is a similar example of the patch approach to the meeting of individual needs in new *interwoven* networks of local partnership. But it is important to recognise that some of those interested in caring for their neighbours may not be keen on joining formal organisations. They may want to undertake their caring quite autonomously, provided they know that help is available when they want it.

Some *good neighbours* with whom I worked for some time made it very clear to me that they did not want to feel *taken over* by local organisations such as the Tenants' Association or by me as a representative of *the welfare*. If I had pressurised them to take on a higher profile within the *patch*, or to join the TA, the very delicate balance of this scheme would have been upset and perhaps they would have withdrawn from any contact with me.

But patch is also sensitive to the importance of the inter-personal dimension in relations between professionals. A close-knit multidisciplinary professional network is often seen as an essential component of good patch work. This is sometimes promoted organisationally by constructing the patch team itself around close working relationships between home helps, wardens, and social workers, as in Normanton (Cooper, 1980, pp. 29–40). In other local authorities close working relationships may have to be promoted more informally.

One specific issue which I was able to address when working in an inner London patch team was the lack of opportunity for home helps to meet with one another as well as with social workers. A regular home help group meeting at the social worker's office helped to resolve both problems by opening up new opportunities for home help/social worker partnership. The same model of multidisciplinary partnership within a specific neighbourhood lies behind the creation of patch liaison links of all kinds. In one team in which I worked all the social workers were responsbile for maintaining specific liaison relationships with a wide range of local professionals and community groups, ranging from a local community newspaper to a number of local GPs. As Cooper argues, 'the set of relationships the team has with other agencies and groups in the neighbourhood is a network in its own right' (Cooper, 1990, p. 29).

The interpersonal and interagency network that linked the patch team to *the local community* was not limited to welfare organisations or welfare professionals. It even extended to people such as the personnel officer of a local hotel. She was very help-ful to us in our attempts to make contact with Filipino hotel workers who were tending to miss out on services. On one occasion I held an advice session in the hotel. Nevertheless, links with commercial organisations are unlike those with welfare organisations. The constraints under which interested or sym-pathetic individuals may be operating, need to be recognised. In this case the hotel was taken over by another company and the whole personnel section was sacked! That was the end of our link with that particular commercial organisation.

Personal relationships are very dependent on trust. This relates to the way in which the pattern of relationships in the patch can reinforce the powers which social workers have or are believed to have. If, for example, people feel obliged to communicate with one another through the patch worker and feel he or she is too influential, the partnership will be in trouble. Because the social

worker has a number of different relationships with different
people suspicion may arise. If a social worker meets local young
people and the local police, the social worker will need to be
very clear with both the young people and the police about the
terms of his or her relationship with them if the partnership with
one or both of them is not to suffer.

I remember quite vividly how one community policeman began to
include our patch office on his regular *beat* and how he spent
longer and longer periods of time in the waiting room chatting to
the receptionists and service users waiting to be seen by us or the
information and advice workers. The effect on our image with local
young people can easily be imagined! He certainly did not intend to
interfere with our work. From his point of view, what he was doing
was simply an extension of his informal liaison relationship with us
and it also gave him an opportunity to *keep his eye on* those who
were coming to see us.

It was not difficult to persuade him that his presence in the
reception area was unhelpful, but for some time it was even more
difficult than usual to persuade some members of the local
community to use our services.

Enabling community

Patch can help people to feel part of a neighbourhood by helping
them to make contact with one another; share things; and work
together towards common goals. Moreover, under some circumstances, local networking can break down artificial barriers
between people and help to develop greater trust and confidence
— an essential ingredient of partnership.

Isolated people placed in bed and breakfast on discharge from
psychiatric hospital can be encouraged to meet — perhaps at a
drop-in. Homeless families living in local hotels can be introduced
to and linked more effectively to services by using the patch
office as a meeting place. Hotel workers from the Filippines can
be offered the opportunity of meeting one another and organised
Filippino groups. Eventually they can be encouraged to express
their own needs and make their own demands on the welfare
system.

Patch social work is also concerned with the quality of
relationships on a patch-wide basis. Certain strategies are oriented
towards encouraging general patch *connectedness*: for example
inviting representatives of different local agencies and community
groups to a *patch lunch* to reinforce patch links. This may help
local professionals and residents to identify with one another and

the local community by sharing food; catching up on local news; and simply being together. One team in which I used to work, held these lunches regularly and they were very useful.

By its very existence, a patch office can encourage inter-dependency. People who identify with the neighbourhood may start to *drop-in* as they go about their daily business in the *patch* (Bennett, 1980, p. 171).

For those who work within it a *patch* can represent a series of opportunities for working together with others. If taken up, these opportunities can bring people closer together and help to build an interdependent patch network.

Mr Ball is about to be discharged from St. Botolph's Psychiatric Hospital which lies inside the Meadow Court *patch*. The hospital based team of community psychiatric nurse, consultant psychiatrist and hospital social worker, are not strangers to the patch social work team because they attend *patch lunches* occasionally, nevertheless they do not know the team very well. Mr Ball's situation therefore presents a practical opportunity for developing closer relationships. The patch social workers seize the opportunity that is presented. One of them sets up planning meetings with Mr Ball, his sister who lives locally, the hospital team, and the manager of the local psychiatric day centre. The meetings overcome suspicions and stimulate a spirit of cooperation and collaboration. They also ensure that Mr Ball's transition from hospital to his flat is relatively smooth.

A few months later, a similar situation arises but this patient is much less cooperative than Mr Ball. Some neighbours have already indicated that they will complain to their MP if the patient returns to his flat to live.

If the professionals had had no prior experience of working together, they might find the complexities of the situation could easily lead to conflict and mutual recrimination. However, having developed the habit of cooperation and some mutual identification as a partnership within the *patch*, this danger is averted.

This example shows how specific partnerships can contribute to the development of a more general patch partnership, charac-terised by increasing levels of interdependency.

But when neighbours are in conflict with one another and in need of support from others in a similar position outside the *neighbourhood*, the patch cannot really be a source of unqualified support. Even without open conflict, the creation of a neigh-bourhood or patch network does not of itself overcome differences of race, class, gender, sexuality, disability/ablebod-iedness, etc — all of which affect relationships between people.

Enabling flexibility and informality

Patch work is both oriented to the informal neighbourhood network and informal in its approach to caring.

Most patch teams attempt to respond to the needs of the
informal caring networks of the neighbourhood by acknowledging that 'it is scarcely surprising that some break down under the
stresses and strains involved' (Barclay, 1982, pp. 199–200).
But the ability to respond to informal neighbourhood networks
is associated with role flexibility. Meeting people on their own
territory in community centres, youth clubs, churches, pubs, and
street corners and listening to what they say about local needs
requires social workers to have a flexible and approachable
manner and to show a real willingness to define their role in
relation to local needs. For what is appropriate in one place may
be inappropriate elsewhere — patch partnerships are constantly
open to renegotiation.

Sometimes informality can lead to role conflict. Many of these
conflicts centre on the issue of power.

On one occasion, I was involved in a mental health assessment on
someone closely related to a person I knew from a local community
organisation with which I was closely involved. The question of
confidentiality could only be resolved by acknowledging that I had a
range of roles within the patch, some of which involved the use of
authority, but that I would respect confidential information and not
share it with others whom we both knew.

There is always potential for role conflict in patch social work. It
is therefore very important for people to be clear about the terms
of their partnership with one another.

Although patch social work puts a strong emphasis on informality, there are limits to the effectiveness of purely local forms of
networking when encouraging and sustaining informality.

Local representatives of different agencies may get on well but
may have to withdraw from collaboration if their respective
hierarchies who are not located in the locality, do not want it to
happen. Policies enacted by agencies may likewise not enable the
development of the kind of flexible roles that members of the
neighbourhood or patch network might wish to develop. Some
neighbourhood networks may not develop the level of *connectedness* needed to create an informal culture within which members
can relate to one another. A local network may still operate with
rigid distinctions between different professionals and between
helpers and those receiving help.

Enabling communication

Strong emphasis in many patch teams is put on getting to know their *patches*. In the case of one patch team that I joined, I was told that for the first three months of its existence, the team concentrated on going out and meeting people and did not declare itself *open for business* until afterwards.

A patch is not just a geographical area but a communication network linking the social work team to a wide range of local individuals, groups, and welfare agencies. It is not there solely to enable social workers to know what is going on locally. It helps to focus the attention of all its members on neighbourhood issues, by providing a context in which all the bits of the local jigsaw puzzle can be put together.

In the patch in which I used to work, it was by talking to one another that teachers, health visitors, social workers, community groups and others discovered that there was an urgent need for a community interpreting service. Everyone realised that those who could not speak English were getting second rate services or no services at all and that a collective effort should be made to establish a new resource which could offer service users a free, flexible and accessible interpreting service.

In this way a communication network is an essential part of the neighbourhood partnership.

Patch communication networks pick up and transmit neighbourhood information. This is useful to identify neighbourhood needs and also to advertise new services. When the interpreting service was ready to start operating, it was advertised by leaflets given to users by a wide range of local agencies and community groups. If anything, these methods were too successful in that by word of mouth, knowledge of the scheme spread so far, that requests were soon received for interpreters from all over London.

Sometimes information gathered on *the grapevine* within a patch can prevent serious mistakes. Currie and Parrott (1986, p. 16) cite the example of a meeting to recruit new foster parents which was to have been held in a pub with an unsavoury reputation, but which was changed to a different venue after the team became aware that this would not be the best place to hold such a meeting.

But *information is power* and it will not always be appropriate to transmit or receive certain kinds of information, particularly the kind of information which could have serious consequences for somebody. An important task for patch social workers is helping to define the rules governing the flow of information around the patch. Perhaps the biggest danger is that the patch becomes a closed circuit of communication and unresponsive to the outside world. All patch workers need to *network* outside the patch to ensure this does not happen.

Enabling action-sets

Patch is concerned with mobilising local resources for local ends. These neighbourhood *action-sets* are not always focused on specific service users: sometimes they are focussed on more general issues. Essentially the mobilisation of patch resources enables people to work together towards specific objectives within the context of a *neighbourhood* or *patch* whether those objectives are defined in terms of individual or collective need.

One of the characteristic ways in which patch *action-sets* are put together is by acting as a *broker*. Where the objective is to channel help to a particular client, network support often involves acting as a *broker* linking the informal caring network to a formal caring network composed of people such as home helps, district nurses but also perhaps local volunteers. It facilitates the *inter-weaving* of all these people and resources. Also it entails developing strong direct links with carers: providing them with information, advice, and emotional support.

Patch brokerage can also be used to describe bringing together any coalition of patch resources by mobilising part of the patch network. This might include, for example developing a lobby for more play facilities for under fives, composed of nursery workers, parents and others. Alternatively, it could be a coalition within the Social Services Department to develop collaboration between the manager of a residential home for elderly people and a home care organiser to campaign for more effective transport for local elderly people. Or it could be a more wide ranging set of individuals or groups brought together around a controversial issue such as local traffic problems.

Brokers play a potentially very powerful role within the context of neighbourhood partnership. Social workers need to be aware of this and ensure that when they take on this role they do not abuse this power.

But, some issues, eg poverty, divorce, etc are likely to link people on a non-neighbourhood basis. Mobilising in *specialist* networks outside the neighbourhood may well be more appropriate to these kind of issues.

Summary

Patch social work has close links with other forms of neigh-bourhood work and shares with them a belief in the value of local *face-to-face* interactions. Although this can be a weakness — and some examples of neighbourhoodism in its pure form show this very clearly — it is also one of its main strengths. Essentially, patch social work is an attempt to *interweave* formal and informal networks within a defined geographical patch to create new localised community partnerships with a number of characteristics:

1. Patch partnerships are localised but wide ranging. They involve a wide range of individuals and agencies active within patch boundaries. Their relationships with one another are a central focus of patch work. Characteristically, patch social workers try to bring all these people closer together by stressing their shared interest in and commitment to the welfare of the neighbourhood. Specific attention is often given to key individuals who can act as neighbourhood *brokers* and help to bring new groups of people into the *patch* network. As with any community partnership, much depends on the personal credibility of patch workers and their ability to inspire trust.

2. Patch partnerships are localised communities. They help to generate a sense of neighbourhood among those who participate and they can also help to overcome isolation. Patch can be empowering. But patch social workers need to remember that the neighbourhood is not always the most meaningful community for some oppressed people.

3. Patch partnerships are developed in the context of an informal *street-level* style of work. Patch workers need to be flexible, even chameleonlike in their choice of roles. This can lead to role conflict. But this in turn can usually be managed. If partnerships are soundly based, they are usually quite resilient.

4. Patch partnerships are local communication systems, which help to make all those involved aware of what is going on in the neighbourhood.

5. Patch partnerships can be seen as neighbourhood *action-sets*. Patch social workers may set up and support specific collaborative projects which may sometimes address the needs of:
   - specific vulnerable individuals;
   - a number of local residents;
   - the patch as a whole.

4 Inter-agency networking

Inter-agency Work

> The term inter-agency work is used to indicate cooperative and collaborative working in joint initiatives by different agencies, both voluntary and statutory... (Hall, 1988, p. 82).

Inter-agency work has been seen as the key to primary health care (Kleizkowski, Elling and Smith, 1984, p. 16); child protection (Maher, 1987, pp. 145–47); and community access to services (Hall, 1988, pp. 82–89). More specifically, the success of community care policy in the UK is linked to the ability of the Health Service and Local Authority Social Services to work together. Likewise, it will not be possible to provide services to *children in need* unless Housing and Social Services Departments find ways of working together.

Inter-agency work has never been more important, but is neither easy nor straightforward. Firstly, we need to know whom to work with. Secondly we need to know how to work with them.

Which partners?

Many inter-agency partnerships are based around a shared interest and involvement with a particular client group. Community Mental Handicap Teams, for example, operate as multidisciplinary networks of social workers, nurses, psychologists, speech therapists, etc seeking to coordinate service delivery. (Humphreys & McGrath, 1986). But the process of deciding which agencies to link up with is not always straightforward. Should only specialist organisations be included? Or should more general welfare organisations which devote a considerable amount of time to the client group also be invited to participate? Should users' groups be included? How might the interests of families and carers be represented?

Even narrowly defined client groups may raise such issues. For example the Joint Planning Teams set up as a forum to discuss issues relating to the care of people with HIV and AIDS are meant to include representatives from Health and Social Services as well as from voluntary organisations. But which ones? No clear answers to this question have been devised and the membership of Joint Planning Teams varies as a result.

Choosing a neighbourhood focus does not always resolve these difficulties. What should determine membership: the address of the agency or its area of activity? What of agencies equally active in more than one locality? Moreover, given that each agency will be likely to define its geographical boundaries somewhat differently, which definition should be adopted as the boundary of the inter-agency network? Sometimes, these issues remain unresolved if for example health service representatives persist in treating what social workers regard as a patch network as a link between the health service and the local authority as a whole.

Inter-agency partnership does not just *happen*. Often, there are real dilemmas involved in the choice of partners. Moreover, having settled on a choice of partners the inter-agency partnership itself needs to be networked.

Enabling interpersonal relationships

Inter-agency links are too easily seen in depersonalised terms. But an inter-agency network brings together people from different organisational *cultures* who need to relate to each other if the network is to be successful.

The potential sensitivity of some inter-agency linkages may mean that all communication needs to be channelled through specific *brokers* nominated by participating agencies. In the early stages, a fragile trust can easily be undermined, if an agency employee unfamiliar with the new *rules* of inter-agency conduct negotiated by brokers acts as if these new 'rules' do not exist. Moreover, although partnership contracts can lay a basis for inter-agency work trust can often only be established on a personal basis. GP/social work liaisons usually require regular meetings between specific social workers and specific GPs. The scope of these liaisons may bear a direct relationship to the level of personal trust established.

Inter-agency links often may be difficult to create and also to maintain. In relationships between local authority Social Services Departments and Health Authorities, trust may be very fragile (Hunter and Wistow, 1987, p. 140) and there is always a danger of *interprofessional demarcation disputes* breaking out (Hill, 1982, p. 73).

Any networking structure designed to promote the integration of the activities of separate but interdependent agencies will consist of pathways linking the agencies. These will pass through certain strategically placed individuals who make use of their interpersonal skills and relationships with one another to keep these pathways open. Therefore it is not only frontline workers who need to develop links with one another. Personal links need to be created and sustained at all organisational levels if the inter-agency link is to function well. Where inter-agency work is successful, it often seems to demonstrate that it is not agencies which relate to one another but people representing them. If large scale bureaucratic organisations are concerned, a constant and skilled brokerage effort is needed to prevent the breakdown of the inter-agency network.

Enabling community

Every organisation has its own culture or established ways of doing things, usually based on its own set of values. Inter-agency networking is therefore a complex intercultural process in which agencies need to develop a sense both of the community they all serve and the community that they themselves have become. This depends on agency representatives making a real effort to empathise with and respect one another's values and perspectives. Helping them to do this involves acting as a cultural broker: helping one partner to see the world through the eyes of the other. As much effort may need to be made with one's own agency as with others to succeed in creating a collective commitment to new practices.

A social worker whom I was supervising gained the rather passive agreement of her team to undertake liaison work with the home care team. Having successfully negotiated an opportunity for social workers to meet specific home helps by appointment at a fixed time of the week, she was dismayed to discover that few social workers were willing to make use of this opportunity. It needed much subsequent work and continual *reminders* to her colleagues to increase the number making use of the new liaison possibilities.

Whether or not a sense of community develops among the members of an inter-agency network depends on the level of *connectedness* or interdependency which has been fostered. Mutual support, for example, is only likely to be a feature of inter-agency relationships if the network is relatively *close-knit*.

Where the only common interest of a number of agencies is referring clients to a social work team, this limited interest could be served by a *loose-knit* network anchored on the social work team as in Figure 3. A, B and C interact with ego on a regular basis but have no direct contact with one another. This might create an efficient referral system, but not a partnership.

But where a number of agencies find much of mutual interest in one another's work then a *loose-knit* structure may well be an inadequate framework for the wide range of contacts each wants. For example, a social work team might decide to link up with other similar teams in an authoritywide network involving information sharing, mutual support, advice and consultation.

One of the patch social work teams in which I worked was involved with other patch teams from the same local authority in regular meetings to learn from one another's experiences and to undertake shared *policy* making. The meeting rotated through the different patch offices and was very much a collective responsibility. This type of network resembles the close-knit network illustrated in Figure 2.

It may be, that if the team involved in the *loose-knit* referral network were to participate in a close-knit network of the kind that has been described, its members might realise that its *loose-knit* referral network is inefficient. Many of the referrals received by the team are simply passed on to other members of the network who could refer directly to one another if the network were more close-knit. Moreover, they might discover that there were many things other than referrals which they could discuss and might even begin to contemplate joint pieces of work.

In establishing a new inter-agency culture it is vital to take account of service user perspectives. The elaborate inter-agency networks that may develop in order to deliver Community Care could become so preoccupied with financial considerations that service quality might slip off the inter-agency agenda. Moreover there may be an assumption that whatever is good for the agencies, ie easiest to organise and deliver is also bound to be good for service users. But we know that service users and agencies may see things very differently (Beresford and Croft, 1980). It needs to be recognised that an inter-agency *community* cannot be said to exist if service users, the *citizens* of that *community* are excluded from it.

Structures need to be developed for inter-agency links to user involvement — not just on agency terms. As Croft and Beresford remind us, people want 'more control over their lives'. This involves playing a genuine role in the decision making process, a process which involves moving from a pre-occupation with 'personal troubles to collective policy' (Croft and Beresford, 1989, p. 16).

Enabling flexibility and informality

Inter-agency work requires flexibility as almost everything has to be negotiated.

The manager of a local authority specialist team for elderly people, might seek to encourage a number of voluntary organisations working with elderly people to join a network to facilitate communication. However, the agencies when contacted might suggest that it would be much more useful to widen the membership criteria to include organisations working with disabled people, as many of the problems faced by these two client groups were similar and many elderly people were also disabled. Moreover, the voluntary agencies might feel that the network would be more useful with a broader content, quickly moving beyond communication to collective supervision of some particularly difficult cases and the development of a range of joint projects.

Negotiation can also narrow the scope of the network partnership. A hard pressed GP may be reluctant to use time which could be devoted to patient care on meetings which resemble a *talking shop*. The GP would be much more likely to join a network of agencies which might make mutual referral easier than one which concentrated on generally reviewing local health needs although such a network might develop over the course of time.

Inter-agency networking usually takes place in the context of a *pattern of existing relationships* (Smale, Tuson et al 1988, p. 15) which may provide the essential building blocks for the future. A link with a local school to improve the quality of referrals; a link with a GP because many clients are registered with her; and a link with a local vicar who wants to start a new volunteer project could all be used as an opportunity for negotiating a broader partnership within a neighbourhood or around the interests of a particular client group.

There is conflict between the bureaucratic mode of organisation and inter-agency networking. Bureaucracy encourages vertical communication up and down the various management levels and strict controls on the transmission of information (Weber, 1978, pp. 956–1005). Networking encourages horizontal communication across organisational boundaries. This can seem threatening. It undermines bureaucratic power and questions rules or assumptions which have never been challenged and which have helped to define organisational *culture* (Schein, 1985). In doing so, it can create an institutional *backlash*. Networkers are easily classified as deviants by those to whom the bureaucratic *status quo* is *sacred*.

Inter-agency networks can create conditions for creative, informal partnerships only if this is linked to some attitudinal change, particularly on the part of senior managers. Individuals have to be empowered to be different and this is something large bureaucratic organisations are not very good at. Service integration will not happen unless agencies are prepared to allow some of their employees to explore new and unfamiliar ways of working. Managers need to be able to contain their anxiety whilst this process of necessary experimentation is going on.

Enabling communication

Inter-agency cooperation cannot flourish without a shared understanding of key issues. For example, a Social Services Department may be seeking to implement a policy of removing suspected abusers rather than their victims from households in which abuse has taken place. But to do this they need cooperation from the Housing Department. If the issue is seen as giving abusers priority over other people on the housing waiting list, it is likely that there will be considerable resistance to the idea both from the Housing Department and those Housing Associations which specialise in accommodation for single people.

Prior to any formal request for cooperation with a policy of removing abusers, representatives of all these agencies should meet to explore the issues and formulate a policy to which they could all feel committed. This process would probably be much more effective if incest survivors or mothers desperate to keep their children out of care had some opportunity for participating in these discussions and making their views known.

Interestingly, it is often a specific issue like this which because it cannot be resolved easily leads agencies to invest time in their relationships with one another. In doing so, they often discover a number of other issues which could be talked about informally and effectively unblock communication over a wide range of subjects which may be of mutual concern. For example, panels set up to discuss the issue of rehousing abusers might also discuss homeless families in particular hotels or elderly people who become homeless as a result of family disputes. If the discussions extended to people recently discharged from psychiatric hospital and placed in bed and breakfast hotels, then the partnership might begin to be extended to include Health Authority representatives. Thus the communication network might continue to grow and evolve.

Enabling action-sets

An inter-agency action-set is a network of agencies involved in some form of collaboration. Almost always, these agencies will have established liaison relationships with one another. To understand the inter-agency action-set process, we need to understand the relationship between liaison and collaboration and as a first step, we need to define our terms.

As words *liaison* and *collaboration* are sometimes used inter-changeably, as if they had the same meaning. But it is probably best to see them as referring to different aspects of inter-agency partnership. It has been argued that they refer to different degrees or levels of partnership.

> Various structures for carrying out networking between organisations can exist: there is a hierarchy, each level being of greater complexity (Payne, 1986b, p. 75).

In this model, organisations can be seen as moving through a number of *stages* in their relationship with one another from *communication*, through *cooperation* and *coordination* to *federation* which is characterised by *interfacing* which includes joint appointments (Payne, 1986b, p. 75).

But a high level of organisational integration, perhaps rather surprisingly, does not in itself seem to necessarily produce an effective inter-agency partnership.

The work of Community Mental Handicap Teams (CMHT), in some areas, appears to have been undermined by the lack of both understanding and ability to work together of the NHS and local authority Social Services, (Humphreys & McGrath, 1986, pp. 21–27). This is even though the teams themselves were organ-isationally integrated, corresponding to Payne's concept of a *federative stage* of development. It has been argued that this shows how important it may be to negotiate partnership by means of *linkage contracts* committing the various organisational hierarchies to the networking effort (Hewitt, 1986, pp. 49–59). Good links between *front line* staff are not enough.

In contrast, networks such as Images, linking small agencies working with young women in Cumbria, or the networks of self help organisations in Holland based around community centres of various kinds (Bakker and Karel, 1983) report few problems in relating to one another. Perhaps this is because these networks are less conflict laden than CMHTs they do not have to find ways of integrating different professional and organisational traditions.

The CMHT experience suggests that rather than seeing liaison and collaboration as different *stages* or *levels* of networking, it may be better to see *liaison* as embodying the continuity of contact between agencies; and *collaboration* as a specific mobil-isation of inter-agency resources. Likewise effective network communication may not be simply the first stage of community partnership but rather the process which underpins the liaison relationship.

The history of the CMHTs and of Joint Planning and Joint Finance (Hunter and Wistow, 1987, pp. 110–156) suggests that

Local Authorities and Health Authorities may not be able to work well with each other in the absence of clear *partnership contracts*. This should give Health Authorities, Social Services Departments and large voluntary organisations pause for thought in their plans for implementing community care. They may need to consider allocating responsibility for developing inter-agency agreements to quite senior managers if *coal face* collaboration is to stand any chance of success.

Liaison links can be used to work out the basis of a future collaboration. The issues which the partnership contract will need to address will depend on the nature of the collaboration.

A contract for an inter-agency project such as a CMHT will need to pay attention to issues such as accountability and line management responsibilities; the resources which will be committed to the project by the various agencies; the proportion of time to be devoted to service delivery as opposed to developmental work; and confidentiality. The purpose of such a contract is to support workers and give them the confidence to develop new ways of working, rather than to impose a new bureaucracy. It is important that this principle is respected — otherwise the contract will be disabling rather than enabling!

But such contracts can never be negotiated once and for all.

An inter-agency *rule* obliged social workers to inform health visitors of any child care concerns or of any new families with young children moving into the area. This rule was constantly flouted by social workers. The health visitors communicated their concern but nothing happened. Discussion within the social work team revealed that people were either unfamiliar with this *rule* or unhappy about it because it appeared to conflict with the professional *rules* about confidentiality. Eventually a new inter-agency code of conduct was negotiated which took account of confidentiality and was respected.

Where inter-agency collaboration is directed towards strategic planning rather than a specific project the contract will need to address a different set of issues.

A community care planning partnership may need to involve a Social Services Department, a Housing Department, a Health Authority, a number of voluntary organisations, service users, and carers. In order to work together they will need to develop a shared understanding of issues such as the roles they are expecting one another to play and the power of the partnership to make decisions which will be binding on all its members.

One of the secrets of developing and then maintaining an effective inter-agency action-set is coordination. But the most appropriate way of coordinating a particular inter-agency partnership will depend on the situation.

One issue is the size of the network. If it is not too big, it may be a good idea to call a network meeting.

A liaison relationship between social workers, community workers, a Tenants' Association, and a local church based group revealed a need for a new youth club on an estate where territorial rivalries effectively made other clubs inaccessible to local young people. A network meeting might enable the partnership to begin work on a campaign to persuade others that a new club was absolutely essential.

The meeting could divide key tasks between different agencies. Community workers might gather and collate evidence of the need and present it to officers and members of the local authority. Social workers might write their own reports commenting on the need for preventative services on an estate with high rates of juvenile crime and young people coming into care. The church based group and the Tenants' Association might contact the local media and persuade them to run stories about the lives of local youngsters and lobby local politicians about the strength of feeling on the estate in support of the campaign. Some network members might seek to broaden the base of the campaign by involving local young people themselves, the police and the probation service. Subsequent meetings could review strategy and develop the campaign as it went along.

But sometimes the inter-agency network will be too complex to enable mobilisation of resources to be undertaken through a single planning meeting.

The development of a mental health resource centre might need to be undertaken by a number of specialist groups, each one concerned with a particular service. For example, the drop-in might be developed by Community Psychiatric Nurses, a volunteer organiser and social workers from local patch teams together with service users. Advice and information services might need to be developed by the Citizens Advice Bureau and community workers. It might be advisable to appoint an overall network coordinator to act as a broker interweaving the different groups into a viable whole.

But network coordinators are not managers and if they possess authority it is only because all those involved are prepared to vest some authority in them.

Summary

Inter-agency networking holds the key to multidisciplinary teamwork and all the other forms of inter-agency cooperation and collaboration which recent developments in social policy are predicated upon. As a community partnership inter-agency work has a number of characteristics.

1. Inter-agency partnerships are *brokered* by individuals occupying strategic positions within their own agencies. Agencies relate to one another through individuals and the success of inter-agency work is dependent on their ability to take their agencies with them into the unknown territory of the partnership. Key individuals have to trust one another. Facilitating inter-agency partnership therefore involves facilitating trust.

2. Inter-agency partnership can be seen as a community process through which the differences between organisational traditions and professional values are accepted. Ways are found to build a sense of common purpose and identity. This requires an ability to relate to and learn from partners whose whole world view may seem very alien, which in turn means dropping stereotypes and preconceptions about them and their work. Wherever possible service users should be brought into this procsss. It needs to be accepted that it is undesirable to submerge their voice within the collectivity of agencies.

3. Inter-agency partnership is concerned with establishing a culture of innovation. It involves developing new services, new ways of working together and very often, new values. In particular, inter-agency partners have to be willing to take risks together and facilitating this is a key networking role.

4. Inter-agency partnership depends upon the development of a set of shared understandings — an effective communication network has to underpin the partnership. Traditional boundaries between agencies may block the free flow of information. A strong emphasis is necessary both in resolving misunderstandings as they occur and setting up channels of communication to develop processes of information exchange.

5. Inter-agency partnership provides a context for the development of inter-agency *action-sets*. It provides opportunities for collective planning and use of resources. The more complex the goals of the partnership, the more important it may be for networkers to facilitate the work of an *action-set*. This can usually be understood as moving from *general liaison* to *specific collaboration* — actively working together on a specific project of some kind. In general liaison may exist without collaboration but not collaboration without liaison. Collaboration is not straightforward and can lead to confusion and frustration. Inter-agency contracts may therefore sometimes be very helpful.

5 Network therapy

Social support network

Network therapy is based on the principle that all of us have a *support system* embedded in our relationships (Caplan, 1974, pp. 1–40). Many so called *personal problems* arise because something has gone wrong with this *support system.*

Several writers have identified the social support network as the key element in social support. Garbarino, for example, defines the *social support network* as

> a set of interconnected relationships among a group of people that provides enduring patterns of nurturance (in any or all forms) and provides contingent reinforcement for efforts to cope with life on a day to day basis (Garbarino, 1983, p. 5).

This suggests that support cannot easily be reduced to any one feature of a social network but is dependent on the interplay of all its characteristics. In particular, Garbarino draws attention to the link between support which is available to individuals and patterns of interaction. In other words, support is seen as a function of network relationships.

Network therapy tends to focus on the implications that this may have for specific individuals identified by themselves or by others as having problems.

Network assembly

If relationships within a network become so distorted that certain individuals experience a loss of support then, it has been argued that any problems that arise as a result can only be resolved by therapeutic intervention at the level of the personal network. The goal of these therapeutic interventions is always to increase social support by helping to create the conditions under which people feel able to enter into a community partnership.

In its original form network therapy is known as *Network Assembly* — a branch of family therapy.

> The social network is a relatively invisible, but at the same time a very real, structure in which an individual, nuclear family or group is embedded. There are malfunctioning social networks as well as malfunctioning families and individuals. The retribalisation goal of social

network intervention attempts to deal with the entire structure by rendering the network visible and viable, and by attempting to restore its function. Thus the social network becomes the unit of treatment or intervention — it becomes the *patient* — and the success or failure of the therapy will require new modes of evaluation (Speck & Attneave, 1973, p. 6).

Network assembly makes a number of far reaching claims which include *resocialisation* of the nuclear family unit within the broader family network; *demystification* of the network; and the removal of pathological network *secrets* and *collusions* by the power of what has been called the *network effect* (Speck & Attneave, 1973, pp. 15–16).

The *Network effect* is essentially a collective experience which Speck and Attneave describe in semimystical terms as *retribalisation* — the rediscovery of a vital element of relationship and pattern that has been lost (Speck & Attneave, 1973, p. 7).

The most interesting aspect of *retribalisation* is that the network is both patient and doctor.

When skilfully harnessed or channelled, this group revives or creates a healthy social matrix, which then deals with the distress and the predicaments of its members far more efficiently, quickly and enduringly than any outside professional can hope to do (Speck & Attneave, 1973, pp. 7–8).

When this is working well 'new feedback connections' are made and 'suddenly no-one is sick' (Speck & Attneave, 1973, p. 10). This leads on to the idea that a *healthy social matrix* will reemerge if the personal network is gathered together.

There are few recorded examples of network assembly in the UK but in the USA it has been more widely used in situations often when the identified patient has been diagnosed as mentally ill or seriously *disturbed* in some way and the immediate family do not feel able to cope. The explanation for its relative unpopularity in the UK probably resides in the time consuming nature of the logistical task; the complexities involved in handling sessions involving large numbers of people; and the fear of losing control of the whole process, as much as in the professional apathy noted by Ballard and Rosser (Ballard and Rosser 1979).

Network assembly has shown that networks are not 'cast in stone' but can be helped to transform themselves in qualitative as well as quantitative terms. Beneath the hyperbole and romanticism lie some very valuable insights about the nature of social support and the dynamics of network change. In its pure form it may be rare. But it can sensitise us to the importance of seeing social networks as a set of complex relationships capable of generating a high level of social support and yet which can *malfunction*. More specifically, it has drawn attention to the problems which can arise within isolated nuclear family units and the possibility of helping such families by assisting them to relocate within a community.

These ideas have a considerable value for practitioners. For example, in some respects case management is a form of network therapy in so far as it is concerned with overcoming isolation and helping the members of the personal *support system* to manage their relationships with one another more effectively. This will be discussed in more detail in the next chapter. But there are even more direct applications for network therapy in work with children and families.

Network therapy: an application to practice

In chapter one, we looked at an example in which the relative isolation of a nuclear family unit provided opportunities for sexual abuse. But isolation can also be antitherapeutic after sexual abuse has been disclosed. If the abuser is removed from the household or agrees to leave, this may reduce risk but in itself does little to enable the family to share the pain, grief, guilt and anger that is likely to be circulating within it. Traditional family therapy or individual counselling may, of course be very helpful and should, in any case, be available. But the family, as a whole may continue to feel isolated and unsupported. The stigma associated with sexual abuse may even make the isolation of the family more pronounced. In a situation like this, network therapy might aim to help the family to reestablish its links with an extended family network and thereby gain an effective informal *support system*. If the abuser is still in the household, the process of reestablishing links with family and friends may be even more important as it would help to increase informal surveillance and thereby reduce the opportunity for further abuse. We can illustrate this by the use of a hypothetical case example.

The Cartwright family appear to be an ideal nuclear family unit. Peter and Paulette Cartwright are married with two children. Peter Cartwright is in regular work and his wife stays at home to look after their two daughters. However, beneath the surface family life is far from ideal. From an early age the daughters now aged 10 and 13 have been sexually abused by their father. Until recently they felt they had little choice but to keep this abuse secret, but they have now told their mother and she has confronted her husband with her knowledge of the abuse. The situation then changes. Peter Cartwright agrees to leave and both social workers and the police become involved with the family. The subsequent investigation reveals a family history of increasing isolation.

Peter Cartwright left home at an early age after an argument with his parents and had little contact with any of his family from then on. After marrying at the age of 18, Paulette Cartwright saw little of her parents or her brothers and sisters. At first, this was mainly her own decision. Her parents had opposed her marriage and her brothers and sisters had supported them. They refused to come to her wedding leading her to say she wanted nothing more to do with them. Moreover, she had always found her mother to be overprotective and was glad of the opportunity to build her own life away from her family. However, later on, Paulette, wanted to reestablish contact with her parents, brothers, and sisters. Peter, however, objected and said it was 'up to them to make the first move'. As a result, she made no effort to contact them. Meanwhile, Peter discouraged Paulette from contact with any of her old friends. He told her she did not need anyone but him.

The family rift became even deeper when Paulette's father died. Peter told her she should not go to the funeral. Paulette was very upset. She wanted to go but did not dare to antagonise Peter, not so much because she was frightened of him, although he had hit her on several occasions but because she was frightened he might leave her when she had no-one else to whom she could turn. Because he made it clear very early on in their marriage that he did not want her to work Paulette had few opportunities to make new friends. After Melanie and Diana were born this isolation got worse. Paulette reacted to this by becoming increasingly dependent on them and discouraged them from visiting friends or going out to ensure that they spent time at home with her. It was in this situation that sexual abuse was initiated and the pathological secrecy surrounding the abuse added to the oppressive claustrophic atmosphere in which the children lived prior to the disclosure of sexual abuse

Intervention

Network therapy is concerned both with the influence of social networks on the way people feel about themselves and with the practical help people can offer one another if the pattern of their relationships allows this to happen. Drawing upon *systems theory*, we may think of the situation in this family, prior to the disclosure of sexual abuse as a kind of unhealthy homeostasis in which both mother and daughters felt isolated and powerless. The disclosure would precipitate a family crisis. But this would also be an opportunity for the development of *new feedback connections* which might help to generate a more *healthy social matrix*. This is the process that network therapy would aim to facilitate.

Giant *network assemblies* described by Speck and Attneave and others may not be the most appropriate form of network intervention. Rather, given the fragility and vulnerability of both Paulette Cartwright and her daughters in this situation, a series of meetings or mini-assemblies between them and other key members of the family might be more useful. A social worker involved with this family might work with all concerned to set up a rolling programme of mini-assemblies until they begin to take on a life of their own.

A meeting between Paulette and her mother might begin to resolve some of the anger and bitterness in their relationship, enough perhaps to enable her mother to assume for the first time her role as grandmother, meeting with her grandchildren and perhaps then even spending time alone with them. This would allow Paulette to meet with some of her old friends once again. Similar meetings might be set up with the girls' aunts and might lead to weekends spent with them enabling Paulette and her daughters to spend time away from the home, all the while rediscovering the 'vital element of relationship and pattern that has been lost'. At the same time the mutual dependency that had grown up between mother and daughters could be gradually replaced by a wider and more heterogeneous set of relationships within which they could all find the pattern of personal support that suited them best. Diana might, for example spend increasing amounts of time with one particular cousin her own age.

Through careful nurturing of ties within the extended network the amount of support available to the family could be dramatically enhanced. This would open up opportunities to talk about the abuse and the powerful feelings it has left — in a context which gives all concerned the strength to cope with it.

Network therapy can also be practised outside the family context and need not be concerned only with reawakening pre-existing relationships. If we think of it in terms of a general concern with the impact of network relationships on the personal support system, then it might include a concern with almost any supportive relationships.

In our example, if Paulette were able to spend time away from her daughters she might be able to think of returning to work or to study. This would be supportive because it would open up new opportunities for her to rediscover her sense of self worth. Network therapy may enable this to happen.

Network therapy as a partnership
Network therapy is concerned with the development of an effective supportive partnership involving not only the social worker/client relationship, but also the relationship between the members of the support network. Like any other partnership it asks of networkers that they address all aspects of the partnership process.

Enabling interpersonal relationships

The essence of network therapy is a concern with social networks as a matrix of potentially supportive relationships and ways of realising this supportive potential. It involves not only a partnership between networker and network but also a partnership between all the members of the potential support network

In our example, this means a community partnership with and between Paulette Cartwright and her daughters and through them the members of the potential support network. This creates the conditions under which the network as a whole can become a partnership. The mini-assemblies in our example help to build this partnership by establishing certain kinds of *linkages* between certain kinds of people. This is only possible, if networkers are attuned to unique possibilities of support inherent in particular relationships. Paulette may obtain practical help and support from her sisters but perhaps receive most emotional support from a particular old friend. Likewise Diana may enjoy being indulged by her newly discovered grandmother but may prefer to talk about her experiences of abuse to a particular cousin.

It is important not to make too many assumptions about who is or who is not likely to be supportive. This is especially relevant when White professionals are working with Black families. Families which deviate from White Anglo-Saxon norms are easily pathologised through a mixture of ignorance and *cultural racism* (Ahmed, 1986, pp. 140–154). Results may be that social workers may either fail to engage family members who could offer support if ways could be found of involving them in a situation or interpret support given from unconventional sources in negative terms. Ahmed gives an example of a White health visitor who, when dealing with an Asian family, felt that in her own words, the three year old son was 'too attached to the grandparents' (Ahmed, 1986, p. 142). Ahmed notes that 'a positive feature of Asian extended family living was ignored (Ahmed, 1986, p. 144). It is not that networkers need to be *cultural experts* but rather that they need to be open-minded and positive in their attitudes and work with people in identifying sources of support. Undertaken in this way, networking can be an antiracist strategy.

People are sometimes highly ambivalent in their attitudes to one another. This is heightened when relationships involve help and support. Nobody likes being dependent on someone else. Offers of help can generate all kinds of fantasies of dependency and powerlessness. Social workers need to be aware of this and address it by ensuring that network relationships are not one-sided and involve as much mutual exchange as possible. When relationships such as that between Paulette and her mother carry a long and painful history, it needs to be recognised that support is a function of the degree to which material has been satisfactorily worked through. Networking needs to provide opportunities to do this: a mini-assembly may also be a counselling session!

Enabling community

Although most personal networks do not have that sense of mutual identification which is a key aspect of any community, there is a sense in which network therapy tends to create a sense of shared purpose. It is artificial but it may be necessary to 'kick start' relationships which may initially have little life of their own. The basis of identification is a shared sense that someone in the network needs help. At first this sense of mutual identification may be little more than an abstraction, but as time passes and relationships develop, the community will become more of an interactional reality. For example, it may be that Paulette Cartwright's sisters had not seen each other for some years, but in trying to offer help to Paulette they may start to meet to discuss the best way of doing so. Setting up mini-assemblies with planning briefs may well be a way for social workers to network a sense of collective purpose.

Working with sexual abuse or indeed many other problems linked to isolation and oppression may be both painful and exhausting. If network members are to sustain their involvement with individuals who may have been profoundly damaged by their experiences, they may need support both directly from a social worker and from one another. Having the two girls to stay may raise all kinds of issues about handling inappropriate sexualised behaviour which Paulette's sisters may want to discuss with one another and the social worker. Opportunities for people to meet and support one another need to form as much a part of the therapeutic plan as direct work with the clients.

In the example, Melanie and Diana might benefit from an opportunity to meet with other young people who have experienced sexual abuse. In this context, it might be possible for them to begin to feel less *abnormal* or wicked than they might otherwise feel if they felt they were the only girls to have experienced this. There might be considerable relief for them in simply being able to confirm that they are not entirely alone in their experience. However supportive their mother might be they may feel unable to talk to her about some of what went on. They might feel more comfortable sharing some of this material with those who could relate to it through their own experience. This process of sharing need not take place in formal group meetings. It could take place at times and in ways that suited Melanie and Diana; in twos or threes; separately or together; face-to-face, or on the telephone or by letter — yet still constitutes a process of mutual support.

To be isolated is to be without choice in relationships and one aspect of networking to overcome isolation — as in our example — is the development of choice. On the one hand this involves developing network resources from which individuals may choose their own support *packages*. On the other hand, the process of working with someone to decide which relationships it may be possible to reactivate and which relationships could be put on a different basis, itself involves choice. In the context of our example, that means Paulette and her daughters having the opportunity to explore network possibilites with a social worker. To have some measure of control over relationships may be, in itself, quite empowering.

Enabling flexibility and informality

Network therapy approaches every situation as a unique configuration of relationships or potential relationships and in that sense it starts with people's problems and situations rather than any overall definition of what a support system should look like. It thus involves an open minded approach and willingness to learn from those directly involved. Networking assumes that people are the real experts on their relationships. Support can be drawn from the most surprising places. Although our example focuses on family ties. It may be that a neighbour or an old friend could be more supportive than a parent, brother, or sister. It all depends on the situation.

Networking is a *needs led* approach. This involves willingness to take on different roles at different times, and an ability to make effective use of all aspects of one's self. So in our example, it may be that Paulette's mother blames her for what happened to the girls. As a result she is rather off-hand with Paulette when they first meet. This leads Paulette to feel even more guilty than before and become depressed. The worker in this situation may need to help Paulette to empower herself by working through her feelings of guilt with her in a careful and sensitive way in order to show her the abuse was Peter's responsibility, not her's. At the same time, Paulette's mother may need to be confronted quite vigorously with the effect her attitudes are having on her daughter. She must understand that this is a chance for her not only to help her daughter and granddaughter, but also to build a new relationship with them. Also that if she carries on blaming her daughter for something for which she was not responsible, she will destroy any possibility of doing this.

Developing a new partnership within the personal support network involves an ability to reach out to potential supporters wherever and whoever they may be. This means being willing to go to where the network is rather than working within some administrative boundary such as that of patch or local authority. Perhaps, even more challenging, it demands of us as professionals, that we are non-judgemental about potential supporters. Sometimes people burdened with debt or with family problems of their own may be uniquely qualified to give support. In our example, one of Paulette's sisters may have had psychiatric problems or a son who has committed a series of petty thefts. This does not mean that she should be ruled out as a source of support for Paulette or the girls. Rather, she may have something to offer them drawn from her life experiences.

Enabling communication

For a support network as in our example, the most important aspect of communication is direct face-to-face communication enabling people to work through their feelings about one another and clarify what it is that they want from one another. In other words good communication is an essential ingredient of support because it enables support to be negotiated. Where relationships are based on fantasies and direct communication reveals that little of value can be gained from them, this harsh but important truth needs to be faced. Networkers need to help all those involved to do this.

Judgements need to be made about how closed or open communication should be. Certain information may be confidential and it is important that those who share information on a basis of confidentiality know who will, and who will not, have access to it. In any therapeutic situation, the rules about confidentiality need to be spelt out. But we should not assume that the same rules apply to everything which is discussed. In our example, it may be that only a therapist and perhaps a social worker have access to detailed information about the way in which Diana and Melanie were abused, but it may be that many other people within the extended family should know that they are feeling lonely and friendless and need to be supported. These issues would need to be discussed with them as part of the work involved in establishing a community partnership which is able to meet their needs.

Once established, a communication network enables support to be mobilised speedily and efficiently. In other words good communication is a vital element in the mobilisation of support for specific purposes in specific action-sets. For example, at some point in the future Paulette may be working full-time. If Melanie falls ill and her mother cannot easily take time off work a message might be passed to her grandmother who could contact one of Melanie's aunts and suggest that they share the responsibility of looking after her.

Enabling action-sets

Network therapy involves working with the pattern of network relationships to facilitate active support. In other words networkers seek to move relationships along a pathway from general expressions of concern through interaction and engagement to more tangible forms of support. It is concerned with helping people to identify how they can relate to one another to begin work with one another. Indeed, the distinction between helping people to relate to one another and helping them to help one another often breaks down in practice. We can illustrate this using our example.

In our example, Paulette reestablishes contact with her mother and sisters. They then become an action-set available to her as a specific network resource; for practical advice; financial help; emotional support; help with looking after her daughters; or new problems which may not have anything to do with the issue of sexual abuse.

In any situation different people will be able to offer different things. One aspect of networking is enabling everyone to sort out what needs doing and who might be best able to do it. The role of the networkers is often to enable the network partnership to emerge by helping all those involved to establish the kind of relationships with one another that make it possible to plan effective help.

But helping to facilitate the coordination of an action-set involves motivating all those concerned to participate in it. Although it is conventional to think of *motivation* in terms of specific rewards, we can also think of it in terms of 'promoting commitment and emotional involvement'. This can be done by helping people to take an active role in decision making (Payne, 1986a, p. 79). Mobilising an effective action-set can therefore only be done on the basis of a strategy of empowerment which takes in the whole partnership. In our example, this might mean ensuring that Paulette's mother and sisters all feel involved in the development of any therapeutic plans.

Summary

Network therapy is based on the principle that the personal network is a *personal support system* and that the effectiveness of this system depends on the pattern of relationships within it. In its pure form it oversimplifies the issues. Support is not just about bringing people closer together. It underplays real conflicts of interest. One can imagine the effect of a network assembly on a young girl whose *disturbed* behaviour may be an attempt to communicate the sexual abuse she may have suffered within the extended family. Nevertheless, as our example shows sexual abuse and other problems can be approached from a social network perspective.

The essential insight of *network therapy* is that the pattern of relationships in a network is like a shifting kaleidoscope which can move from an unsupportive or *malfunctioning* pattern to a more supportive pattern. This is a model of partnership which focuses on the supportive potential of a range of informal social relationships. It can be summarised as follows:

1. Therapeutic partnerships focus on the dynamics of interpersonal relationships — conflicts between individuals; the ambivalent feelings people may have about one another; and the tension between independence and dependence within a personal network. Mini-assemblies of two or more people can be used to work through these issues.

2. Therapeutic partnerships can generate a sense of community. They can overcome isolation; help people to identify with others in the network; provide opportunities for mutual support. For those who have been isolated they can provide choices about relationships and therefore a new control over them. Getting people together in mini-assemblies can help to build a sense of community which may not have existed before.

3. A therapeutic partnership starts from where the network is. It explores the supportive potential of an existing set of relationships and the obstacles to support in that set, and makes use of the insights of those who are personally involved. Network therapy should not impose a fixed idea of a *healthy* set of relationships. It is best described as an organic strategy for developing supportive partnerships.

4. Therapeutic partnerships can be facilitated by reducing miscommunication. Opportunities for direct face-to-face communication help to counteract blaming, avoidance, projection, or the general tendency people have of fantasising about one another, particularly at times of crisis. All of these things distort relationships and undermine the supportiveness of network relationships. Communication networking is therefore very much a part of network therapy.

5. Therapeutic partnerships are concerned with helping social networks to transform themselves into therapeutic *action-sets*. They are concerned with helping members of personal networks to see how they might collaborate with other members to interact more positively with help-seekers. To this end, facilitating coordination of offers of help to have an optimum impact on problems can be seen as a therapeutic intervention. This can only be done if helpers feel genuinely involved in the therapeutic work.

6 Case management and community care

Case management and social support

Case management and network therapy share a concern with developing the strengths of the *social support network*. Whereas network therapists have been preoccupied with the dynamics of extended family networks, case managers have been concerned with the effective coordination of both formal and informal care services. In most people's minds case management is synonymous with community care. Although this chapter will focus mainly on community care issues, the case management approach is applicable to a wide range of situations and problems.

Case management has been described as 'a mechanism for linking and coordinating segments of a service delivery system (within a single agency or involving several providers)' (Austin, 1983, p. 16); or as the development of *service* or *care packages* to meet the needs of particular individuals (Steinberg and Carter, 1984, p. xi). This involves needs' assessment; a database containing information about relevant services; and a process by which appropriate resources can be linked with one another and the informal services provided by family and friends. Case management involves a whole range of activities which contribute to this process. Nevertheless, all are based on the principle that care should be *needs led*: seen as a whole and from the point of view of the service user rather than the service providers.

Care packaging and service menus

A *care package* is a specific set of services put together from a much wider range of service options which in contemporary *computerspeak* are sometimes referred to as the service *menu*. Service *menus* can only be created in the context of an effective interagency partnership which will clarify the terms under which representatives of these agencies will be able and willing to work together. A service *menu* is the set of interagency contracts which this process produces (*see* Chapter 4). It is put together by a *lead agency* which is responsible for taking a planning initiative. In most cases the lead *agency* and the case management agency are one and the same.

The pattern of interagency contracting which creates the *service menu* will tend to reflect the way in which the *lead agency* or case management agency operates, both through its organisational structure and its general professional orientation.

A disabled single mother and her six month old child who recently moved into a new flat on an unfamiliar housing estate might be in danger of losing contact with her informal support network at the other end of the borough and need a range of coordinated *formal* services. However she might receive a different *package of services* if her local Social Services Department was committed to a patch philosophy rather than a specialist model of social work.

The patch social worker's care package might focus on building a new informal network on the estate as well as encouraging old friends to continue seeing her. In addition the social worker might attempt to link her with local women's groups, medical facilities, playgroups etc, and arrange for a local home help to visit to help with cleaning.

A social worker specialising in problems of disability on a boroughwide basis might also encourage the client's old friends to keep in contact with her and might link her with the same local GP and health visitor. More emphasis might be put on linking the client to a range of specialist resources such as a disability action group, a counsellor specialising in work with disabled parents, and a specialist support worker to help with a range of tasks in the home.

The difference between these *packages* reflects variation in the kind of service *menus* used by patch based teams and specialist teams. As there will be strengths and weaknesses in all of them diverse *menus* may not be a problem. However, if case management is to be an empowering process, service users and carers should be enabled to intervene in the development of service 'menus' to ensure that they are not wholly dependent upon professional perspectives. Self advocacy groups and networks need to be given a role in the developmental process.

The concept of a *menu*, irresistably brings to mind the image of a restaurant. If we follow this through, as a metaphor, then service users and carers need to be involved in choosing what will go on the menu as well as what they have for lunch!

Interweaving care
In the context of community care the language of case management or care management often seems to imply that it is a rather technocratic, managerial and cold blooded exercise. *Packaging* of

care is dependent on an ability to work with clients and *informal carers* (Steinberg & Carter, 1984, pp. 25–26) as well as with representatives of other agencies. It could well be described as an *interweaving* strategy of the kind advocated originally in the *Seebohm Report* and elaborated upon in the *Barclay Report*.

Interweaving cannot be accomplished at a desk or computer terminal because it is dependent on *face-to-face* communication and negotiation with clients and carers (Bayley, 1973, pp. 316–317). Unfortunately, many of the debates about case management or care management in the UK do not appear to acknowledge this. In particular, it is proposed that case management should be a market driven system in which *value for money* will lead automatically to service quality. This is a deeply flawed idea.

Care markets and caring networks

Following the publication of the *Griffiths Report* (Griffiths, 1988), the subsequent White Paper, Caring for People and the passing of the *NHS and Community Care Act* (1990), Social Services Departments have been encouraged to see case management or care management as a way of importing market disciplines into the personal social services. This has been seen as facilitating the *networking of services* (Laming, 1989, p. 19). But networking is not a market activity. Markets generate competition. Networking generates cooperation.

If we consider the impact of market forces on the nature of *service menus*, 'enlightened self-interest' will result in an emphasis upon services with wide profit margins and a retreat from services with a high level of financial risk attached to them. This can only reduce choice and undermine the principle of a *needs led* service.

In relation to the interweaving of care, commercial style contracts with detailed service specifications will be very difficult to combine with the growth of organic interdependence and collective decision making associated with networking. As a result, far from encouraging power sharing, such contracts would tend to increase the power of the case manager, as only he or she would really know what the whole picture of care was.

As far as welfare professionals are concerned, if human need is transformed into a set of market opportunities, then the structural opposition between buyer and seller and the competition between service providers for as large a slice as possible of any particular market is bound to take its toll on the nature of their relationships with one another.

As far as service users are concerned, their relationship with service providers is likely to be constrained by having to develop within the confines of a rigid *service specification*. The flexibility valued by clients and interpreted as evidence of genuine caring will not exist. Also it is much easier to cost things which are done for someone than with them. Doing things with someone involves the time and effort of making a relationship, it is easy to see how service contracts might emphasise the practical and the mechanical at the expense of the relationship. There is a real danger that far from promoting *quality*, contracts which are tightly specified will stifle innovation and flexibility (Bamford, 1990).

Separating care purchasing from service provision is supposed to ensure that case management is needs-led. If this means that all power is in the hands of someone who is not in direct contact with service users then they may have even less opportunity to influence the nature of their own care.

Market principles could combine with managerialism in ways which could lead case management to oppress rather than empower service users.

> The danger of over-emphasis on management control of care systems lies in dismantling individual power systems. While management is important, collaboration is also of the essence, and it is collaboration with all parties at all stages, which holds the key to the provision of community care without revoking individual power and responsibility (Collins, 1989).

Markets may serve all kinds of useful purposes, but they do not encourage people to listen to or support one another. This is vital for all those involved in working with and caring for vulnerable people. In addition, if asking for help is to be seen as failing to have delivered according to the terms of a service contract, then no one will ask for help or express uncertainty — a recipe for disaster rather than good practice.

Perhaps the biggest danger in a market driven version of case management is that in the rush to develop an *enterprise culture* within the personal social services we may create a system which is so constrained by budgetary considerations that it is almost entirely reactive: offering help to only the most vulnerable individuals and those *informal* networks which are on the brink of collapse.

Alternative model of case management

Even if markets and the concept of *value for money* have a place in case management, they cannot in themselves generate community partnership. This requires a different approach.

Enabling interpersonal relationships

Quality in community care cannot be reduced to *cost effectiveness* or even *value for money*. This is because the effective coordination of a support network involves paying attention to the quality of all its links over a period of time — not just the quality of individual services at any one moment. It means paying attention to the way people feel about one another and themselves.

If the needs of informal or formal supporters are ignored service quality will suffer. Carers are often unable to meet dependency needs because they themselves do not feel sufficiently cared for or valued (Nissel and Bonnerjea 1982). *Caring for the carers* has therefore to be a basic principle of case management. Support groups, respite care, home care support to help with domestic tasks, and perhaps the allocation of a social worker specifically to carers are all services which case managers can use to turn this principle into a reality.

Professionals too, can sometimes feel very alone with their problems and here the relationship between the case manager and one or more of the service providers may be the critical factor.

Emily Francombe is an eighty-seven year old woman living alone in a bed-sit owned by a housing association. She is rather confused and very suspicious of others. She is convinced her neighbours are plotting against her and sometimes directly accuses them of this. Her mental and physical health continue to deteriorate until she stops paying her rent, regularly loses her pension book, and sometimes goes without food for some days.

The housing association makes a referral to the Social Services Department and a social worker tries to visit. At first, Emily refuses to open the door, but eventually the social worker gains access to the bed-sit. After several months of visiting he manages to persuade Ms Francombe to accept a home help. However, although she allows the home help to visit she will not allow her to do any cleaning, only some minimal shopping, and if she is ill or on holiday refuses to allow any other home help into the flat. The social worker continues to visit but only every couple of weeks and the day-to-day monitoring of the situation is almost entirely dependent on the home help.

The GP, social worker, and community psychiatric nurse all agree that the home help should continue to visit Emily Francombe in spite of the limitations placed on her. But the home help has to cope with an enormous amount of stress, as a result of these visits. Sometimes, Ms Francombe refuses to allow her into the bed-sit; sometimes she allows her in but cross-questions her about her movements; sometimes she subjects her to long lists of complaints about her neighbours; and because of her short-term memory loss, she almost always asks her the same questions over and over again. If the home help is to be enabled to continue her work she, herself, will need some help.

The social worker, quickly realises that there is little point in visitng more frequently himself. This would do little to ease the stresses and strains for the home help. Instead, he offers to see the home help for a regular consultation session, designed to provide the kind of additional support and assistance which would enable her to carry on.

This is an example of the way in which case managers can sometimes address care issues most effectively through indirect strategies such as consultation.

Case management is as much about supporting those doing the caring as it is about planning and coordinating care. In this case, the care package involves a very small number of people but this does not mean that the case management task is a simple one. If the case manager had ignored the home help's needs, it is likely that her morale would have deteriorated to the point where the very fragile care arrangements which had been made for Emily Francombe would have collapsed.

Enabling community

If those who are involved in caring for someone are to establish a successful partnership, they sometimes need to meet on a face-to-face basis. Especially when the stresses and strains of caring lead those involved to feel frustrated and angry with one another and to search for someone to blame. Projection of bad feelings around the network is a sure sign that the support system has become overloaded with anxiety and that its members need to be helped to come together not only to make new plans but to enable individual members to feel part of a collective effort — a community which will care for all its members and not only for the client.

This is the process of *network conferencing* which in some ways is rather reminiscent of the therapeutic technique of *network assembly* described in the previous chapter. It has for some time been recognised that *network conferences* are an important case management tool (Steinberg & Carter, 1984, p. 23). However, they should not only be seen as a way of working with the informal network to enhance self-sufficiency. I have elsewhere described conferencing as 'a way of structuring time and structuring relationships in order to enable the network system to move out of a position of crisis' (Trevillion, 1988, p. 302). This example shows these principles at work in an *interwoven* rather than a purely *informal* network.

Jean Jackson was a seventy-five year old woman cared for by her niece, a home help, her GP and the staff of a psychogeriatric day centre. For some time this network was able to care adequately for Ms Jackson without any outside intervention. I first became involved after a series of increasingly anxious telephone calls came through to my team about Ms Jackson which made it clear that members of the caring network felt unable to cope with what they perceived to be a rapidly deteriorating situation. This message was couched in terms of a request for an assessment under the terms of the *Mental Health Act*.

At first, I was in no position to make any judgements about Ms Jackson's mental health beyond the fact that it was obviously a cause for concern. But two issues were clear to me. Firstly, there seemed to be little or no communication between different members of the existing caring network. Secondly, all those telephoning and speaking to me or other members of my social work team were convinced that we were faced with an emergency situation but they all found it very difficult to say of what exactly the crisis consisted.

After, I had spoken directly to Ms Jackson and a consultant psychiatrist it became clear to me that Ms Jackson was suffering from Alzheimer's disease but her mental state was not deteriorating significantly. This suggested to me that the key issues might lie elsewhere.

My response was to call a series of network conferences which I would chair and to which all the carers and a number of managers were invited with the purpose of assessing the nature of the perceived crisis. Although there was considerable initial opposition to this strategy from some members of the network who felt that we should be acting rather than 'wasting time' talking, anxiety levels began to drop almost as soon as a network conference was scheduled. So much so, that the conference itself was almost an anticlimax!

When we met, it became apparent that all the carers, both professional and non-professional felt rather isolated from one another. An opportunity to meet helped them to begin sharing with each other and with me some of their frustrations and anxieties. The conference in other words began to build new mutual support mechanisms where before there had been none. It also began to clarify the boundaries of responsibility for every member of the conference so that caring became a more manageable and less personally oppressive activity. Most importantly, conferencing the problem rather than admitting Ms. Jackson to a psychiatric ward, counteracted the sense of personal failure felt by all those concerned and substituted for it a sense of collective strength.

Network conferencing is an example of how case management needs to address the fact that the dynamics of the *social support system* are as much a part of the *care package* as the separate bits of that *system*.

Network conferences empower carers but it is possible that the wishes of vulnerable or inarticulate clients could be compromised in this process. Efforts should be made to involve service users in conferences wherever possible. This may not always be possible. One might imagine that in the case of Ms Francombe a conference might have felt so threatening and frightening that it would have been counterproductive to have involved her directly in one. But in most cases, it will be possible to involve people to some degree, even if this means dividing the conference into two parts. A mentally distressed service user may only have to deal with people well known to him or her but the conference process can nevertheless also include relevant managers and others either before or after this informal conference.

Community care is not just about services or ways of responding to problems, it is also about helping people to lead the kind of lives that they want to live with as many options as possible available. Therefore it is not only caring partnerships that need to be networked, but partnerships for living. This cannot be accomplished without involving service users.

Although it could be argued that case management should be concerned only with specific care problems, this cannot be done without reference to the part played by the *structure of living* — largely self sustaining patterns of informal network support embedded in everyday social interactions (Bayley, 1973, p. 316). In planning for care on a preventative basis, case managers inevitably get involved alongside service users, in what one could call *lifestyle* decisions.

Day has suggested that different kinds of support network provide different kinds of *opportunities*. In relation to a study of people with learning difficulties he has divided these into a *segregated* type and a type of network that allows the handicapped person access to the *non-handicapped world* (Day, 1988, p. 277). The implication is that all those involved in *normalisation* work are to some extent involved in the preventative aspects of the case management process and that residential workers as well as field workers could therefore lay claim to a role in this.

There is also another implication. Services affect people's lives — not just their ability to cope. Case managers therefore need to ask themselves not only whether a set of services will help people to *cope* but also whether they add to the quality of life. Service users may feel that some risks may be worth running if they improve the quality of life!

Enabling flexibility and informality

As we have already seen, case management is very dependent on the context in which it is practised. Moreover effective case management depends upon ability to respond to the demands of a situation rather than to impose a fixed formula of care upon it. It is probably best to see case management as embracing a continuum of caring partnerships rather than as a single activity.

At one end of the case management continuum are those situations where the informal network is in difficulty but might with advice, information and support from a case manager, be able to cope. But even here the relationships between those involved and their feelings about themselves and what they are doing may need to be explored as well. People may not want or need formal services but feel overwhelmed with anxiety and or feelings of guilt that they are not doing more.

Case managers can offer a real service simply by listening to carers and confirming that there is nothing more that they can do.

A woman may have been caring for her mother with the help of a neighbour for some years. Eventually, her mother's health may start to deteriorate and relationships between herself, her mother and the neighbour may become more difficult than in the past. Although she does not yet feel that additional services are needed and not want any kind of direct social work intervention, she may contact a case manager to request information about domiciliary and residential care services. This should be given, but her own needs should also be identified and addressed, at the same time. It will help her to recognise that some things are inevitable and if her mother does eventually need more help it will not be because she has failed. If she feels less anxious and more accepting of her own needs and limitations, the daughter is likely to feel more positive about what she is doing. It is likely that this will enable her to handle her relationship with her mother and the neighbour more confidently and successfully than in the past.

At the other end of the case management continuum are those situations where there is a small or non-existent informal caring network and case management is concerned with establishing a *care package* provided by representatives of a number of welfare agencies. Ms Francombe (*see* above) is an example of this. But in many cases the *care package* might be much more complex, in addition to a social worker and a home help, there might be a need to link district nurses, community psychiatric nurses, volunteers, occupational therapists, day centre workers and others together in an effective partnership.

In the middle of the case management continuum are *interwoven* networks consisting of *informal* and *formal* components where the aim is to enhance informal *structures for coping*.

> A young woman with learning difficulties and severe behavioural problems cannot be left alone. But the family may be able to continue caring for her with regular respite care and night 'sitters' coordinated by the case manager.

An informal and flexible style on the part of the worker is particularly important when trying to build an *interwoven* network or hold one together.

It is important to stress that it is not the needs of an individual which determine the nature of case management but rather the relationship between needs and resources in a particular situation. In other words, the needs which case management addresses are situational rather than individual.

> A young man with severe learning difficulties may have an active social life and a supportive extended family which means that his periodic difficulties in living can be overcome either without any outside intervention or with minimal case management. The same young man living in an isolated nuclear family with few friends and two parents in poor health is more likely to have unmet needs leading to frustration and perhaps even violence which means that his needs may only be met by an 'interwoven' support network of some kind providing the same level of resources as were available informally in the other situation.

Enabling communication

A case management system is a communication network. Through this network messages are transmitted from case managers to service providers, from one service provider to another, and from service users to both service providers and case managers. One way of evaluating case management is in terms of the speed and clarity with which all those involved can communicate with one another about needs and resources, and problems in matching them. A key factor is the case manager's own skills in communication networking.

Case management is an exchange system in which information is passed from one person to another in the expectation that all those who give information will also receive it. The quality of mutual understanding tends to improve over time as a direct consequence of the process of exchanging information. In other words, people are more likely to listen to one another in the future if they feel that information has not been kept from them in the past.

If Mr Bloch, an eighty year old man, some years after the death of his wife begins to feel anxious about continuing to live alone and asks to see a social worker, it is very important that he is helped to make a *positive choice* (Wagner 1988) about his future. As he is given more information about the range of services which might be available to help him, it is likely that he will divulge more and more about any problems of daily living that he might be experiencing. He may also disclose more and more information about his fears and anxieties. As time passes the exchange of information creates a positive feedback effect in that the exchange relationship itself will begin to enhance the quality of communication. When the social worker outlines the kind of consequences that might arise from a move to a residential home, Mr Bloch listens. At the beginning of their relationship, he might have been inclined to interpret this information as simply a bit of bureaucratic nonsense designed to stop him getting the service that he wants. But he now knows that this social worker has told him the truth in the past and is likely to be telling him these things, with his best interests in mind.

We cannot divorce communication from trust and personal credibility. This is why communication has to rest on partnership principles.

Mr Bloch is visited by a GP, a district nurse, a neighbour and a niece. They all know him but they do not really know one another. When the niece hears from the case manager that the neighbour feels that her uncle cannot go on living at home any more, her first reaction is to dismiss this as an unwarranted intrusion into family business. However if the case manager provides an opportunity for her to meet with the neighbour and hear from her some worrying information such as the fact that on several occasions during the past month Mr Bloch has fallen in the kitchen, she may begin to revise her opinion and tell the neighbour and the case manager that on several occasions her uncle has forgotten to turn off the gas cooker after supper. She had thought these were isolated incidents but they now seem part of a pattern. When the neighbour and the niece get in contact with the district nurse and they comment on how much more anxious Mr Bloch has become over the past few months, they all begin to realise that there is a general pattern of increasing frailty, confusion and unhappiness which they all need to address.

At this point it begins to make sense to talk in terms of communication at the level of the whole network. At the network level, individuals gain access to the overall case management picture which enables them to transcend their own, inevitably partial view of the situation and identify the pattern of needs and therefore the pattern of services which they need to deliver collectively. Facilitating communication at a network level is an important aspect of case management.

Enabling action-sets

The effectiveness of any case management partnership is ultimately measured by its capacity to deliver an appropriate blend of informal and formal services in a reliable and efficient manner. Case management is primarily a strategy for mobilising support: the case management partnership is primarily an action-set. Sometimes, people act as if case management consisted of simply asking people to deliver a particular service or, if necessary persuading them to do so. But case management is often less about persuading people to do things than persuading them to do them together. An example may help to illustrate this.

Ms Winkler, an eighty-five year old woman of central European origins, lived alone in a flat which is badly in need of major repairs. She had lived with a female friend for many years. After her friend died she became depressed and withdrawn. She ventured out less and less and by the time the case manager became involved, her increasing frailty was beginning to make it very difficult for her to continue living on her own. She was initially reluctant to have a home help or to see anyone other than the case manager. At first, the case manager believed she was totally isolated, but although she was alienated from her family and had few friends, he/she soon discovered that certain other people were interested in her welfare.

For some years she was had intermittent contact with a small voluntary organisation. Someone from this organisation was very willing to be involved in the future. Likewise, her GP was very concerned about her and keen to help as much as he could. Someone who worked in the garage opposite her flat bought her a newspaper a couple of times a week and like the others was interested in her future welfare. The problem was not mobilising support. That seemed to be surprisingly easy. The problem was persuading these potential helpers to coordinate their efforts.

Action planning began with a network conference which started to develop some sense of collective identity, even though the mechanic did not attend. However, it quickly became clear that a coordinated effort would only be possible if people feel that by giving up some of their autonomy and therefore some of their individual power they are to gain some real collective power. Tasks should not be imposed on them but rather emerge from a process of negotiation with one another. Without this everyone would continue to go their own way — in effect there would be no case management.

In this example, the case manager was successful in persuading people to trade their ineffective autonomy for an effective partnership. The mechanic agreed to ensure that he saw Ms Winkler whenever he delivered the daily newspaper and to contact the case manager if she did not appear when he knocked. The GP and the welfare worker from the voluntary agency agreed to continue to visit once a month but on a new pattern so Ms Winkler saw one of them at least once every two weeks. The case manager arranged to visit every two weeks but never on the same week as either the GP or the welfare worker. In this way the partnership was able to develop an initial set of services which consisted of a daily *early warning* system and weekly contact with everyone else.

As time passed it became possible to introduce new services such as a district nurse and a home help. After patient negotiation with Ms Winkler arrangements for her to attend a day centre on a weekly basis were made. New services were only introduced at a pace which was determined by Ms Winkler herself and in ways which fitted in with the existing *package*.

Summary

Case management is concerned with the coordination of social support. It encompasses a wide range of activities and client groups but is closely associated with community care: in particular the coordination of *care packages*. A major focus of case management is the *interweaving* of the content of these *packages* of formal services with the activities of the informal support network.

At the moment the dominant model of case management/care management is a market model. But market competition and a private sector management style cannot by themselves create an atmosphere of cooperation and mutual support nor a willingness to listen to service users and carers. Only a partnership based case management practice can do this.

1. Case management partnerships are responsive to the significance of interpersonal relationships. Partnership involves recognising that social support is a function of relationships as well as being a set of services. In particular, a major focus of the work of the partnership is often on the resolution of issues of dependence/independence for service users, and issues of conflict and cooperation between service providers. Case managers need to see part of their role as facilitating these processes.
2. Case management partnerships are caring communities. They can overcome isolation, develop their own collective identity, and provide a context for collective effort. Network conferences

to be shared; and stimulate mutual support among members of the partnership. Moreover, in this way they can make the partnership itself more of a reality. By enabling service users to express their choices network conferences can empower them and their carers showing all concerned that case management is concerned with the lives of people and not just the mechanics of service delivery.

3. Case management partnerships are as varied as the pattern of community care. This includes anything from advice and information to a comprehensive *package* of formal services with a whole range of *interwoven* structures in-between. All of these have different partnership implications. Case management is or should be an holistic response to a situation. This means that needs are defined flexibly according to the nature of the situation. The way in which care is *packaged* should reflect this. The best kind of case management is led by the demands of the situation, and the needs of individuals. It is not predetermined by concepts of role and expertise or rigid distinctions between professionals and non-professionals, helpers and helped. Therefore, in setting up partnerships, case managers should adopt a *needs led* approach.

4. Case management partnership involves sharing information. Those who are working together to provide care need to have access to relevant information. In this context, confidentiality should be seen as a set of rules for the dissemination of information. Effective communication also means that people have to be able to listen to one another. This involves trust and the establishment of positive relationships. When information starts to flow around a network a new level of communication is reached, whereby a variety of perspectives on case management issues becomes available to members of the partnership. Case managers can help to facilitate all these processes.

5. Case management partnership is about coordinating and collectivising action. It involves exchanging the apparent autonomy of isolated and unsupported acts of caring for the much more real sense of control which comes with being part of a team. This is the principle that case managers constantly seek to promote and they do so in tangible ways by facilitating negotiations about who should do what, with whom should they do it, and when or how often should it be done. Through these negotiations the case management partnership comes together as an action-set.

7 Self-help, self-advocacy and empowerment

Political is personal

Radical social workers have sometimes tended to prefer the abstractions of class struggle (Bennington, 1970, p. 6) to a genuine engagement with the experiences of oppressed people. Thankfully, in the wake of feminism we are now able to recognise that oppression is always both personal and political.

At a personal level, powerlessness is associated with lack of choice not only about the kind of life one wants to lead but also about the kind of person one wants to be. Classic studies of powerlessness within *total institutions* (Goffman, 1968 and Foucault 1979) have shown how the *rituals, regimes* and *disciplines* of these places can determine every aspect of the lives of their inmates. This even extends into the image that inmates may have of themselves. In Goffman's memorable phrase there is within the *total institution* a 'mortification or curtailment of the self' (Goffman, 1968, p. 50) which may make it impossible to even contemplate resistance.

As a result of these studies we know that the exercise of power is related to an ability to isolate people from one another except on terms dictated by those who hold power as in a kind of totalitarian distopia.

> The prison must be the microcosm of a perfect society in which individuals are isolated in their moral existence, but in which they come together in a strict hierarchical framework, with no lateral relation, communication being possible only in a vertical direction (Foucault, 1979, p. 238)

To be denied the opportunity to communicate about one's powerlessness with others who are in the same position is the most fundamental characteristic of oppression. Within our society many of those who are disadvantaged or discriminated against on grounds of race, gender, class, age, disability, or sexuality may also be isolated from those who are similarly oppressed. In particular, many users of welfare services fall into this category of the isolated oppressed — those who are isolated in their oppression and oppressed by their isolation. For them empowerment starts with the discovery that they are not alone.

Communities of interest

The term *community of interest* can be used to describe a wide range of *networks of relationships* and the *allegiances* associated with them (Barclay, 1982, pp. xiii). But this is rather too broad. For example, family networks are sometimes spoken of as if they were a *community of interest* but, as anyone working with families will recognise, family members may well have very different *interests*.

I will therefore use it in a more restricted sense to mean a social network which develops around an awareness of oppression.

A *community of interest* is not an abstract concept. It is a real process of interaction with others with whom one identifies. If this process of interaction and mutual identification is not present we can, at best, only talk about a potential *community of interest*. All the Black social workers employed by a Social Services Department constitute a potential *community of interest* given that they may have in common experiences of personal and institutional racism. But only those for whom 'Blackness' is subjectively meaningful, and who are able to perceive race as an oppression are likely to seek to form relationships with one another to combat racism within the Department.

A community of interest can only ever address one aspect of our social identity. Therefore any community of interest will contain within it a wide range of other *interests*. To survive and flourish communities of interest need to establish themselves as partnerships in which the sources of difference and even conflict are recognised but in which the sources of collective identity are given priority. These communities are not *natural*. As new issues or needs are discovered so too new communities arise in what is essentially a political response. We can illustrate this by looking at one of the newest *communities* in the UK those living with or affected by HIV and AIDS.

HIV and AIDS: a new community

The failure of established medical and social work services to respond adequately to the new pattern of needs associated with HIV and AIDS led to the development of a wide range of self-help groups some of which later developed organisational features (Alperin and Richie, 1989, p. 170). In the USA it has been found that the typical community based AIDS service organisation was a voluntary, not for profit, non sectarian, free standing organisation that started as a support group (Alperin & Richie 1989, p. 166).

This could also be a description of UK organisations such as Body Positive or Positively Women. They are unconventional organisations. They have grown out of a community's discovery of itself and its power to challenge official neglect and media inspired *moral panic* (Vass 1986, pp. 18–75). They developed their own services to suit their own needs. One of the most important legacies of the early emphasis on self-help for all those currently involved in work with people living with HIV has been the belief that services should be made to fit people rather than people to fit services.

The new community which has grown up in response to the spread of HIV infection provides a striking demonstration of the effectiveness of at least some forms of self-help. The decline in the rate of new HIV infection in the gay community has been in large part because of a massive swing to safe sex practices (Fitzpatrick, et al 1989) probably promoted more effectively by personal contact than by government education programmes. The lack of any comparable educational network among young heterosexual men and women (National Youth Bureau 1988, pp. 3–4) has meant that in spite of government publicity, there is an increasing rate of infection among heterosexual men and women, first noted in the USA (Ryan, 1987, p. 2).

Oppression, resistance and networking

All the major social movements of our time are the result of people networking to empower themselves. Feminism, antiracism, gay rights, antiageism, disability activism, etc are all based on links forged in, through and for collective acts of resistance.

The *web of women* created, sustained and mobilised at Greenham Common Cruise Missile Base is a good example of this. The image of the web was the symbol of the Greenham Common Peace Women. It was also the symbol of the national and international feminist network of sympathisers and activists which sustained the Peace Camp. It enabled a relatively small and often quite vulnerable group of *campers* to be transformed at times into a massive demonstration by women capable of encircling the base.

If Greenham Women could be found all over the world, other acts of resistance are much more localised. Although we need to distinguish between *local communities* and *communities of interest* (Barclay, 1982, p. xiii) it is often at a local level that it is easiest for oppressed people to network with one another. This is particularly so for elderly or disabled people. One example might be a local network of disabled people linking up with one another to persuade the local authority to provide some appropriate transport to enable them to get to the shops.

Social work, self-help and social change

The relationship between self-help and social work is highly complex. There are many different forms of self-help all needing a different kind of response from the social worker (Adams, 1990, pp. 26–36). From another point of view, the issue is relatively straightforward. Social workers should always facilitate self-help, but the most appropriate way of doing so will depend on the nature of the situation. In that sense it is no less and no more complicated than any other aspect of practice.

We can all agree that social workers can help to facilitate self-help by 'building groups and networks to promote long term solutions to people's powerlessness' (Edwards, 1988, p. 39). But it is vital to remember that it is self-helpers who need to work with one another and the role of the social worker or community worker is only to facilitate this. The social worker may help the community to come together but is not a part of the community and should not pretend to be!

In relation to HIV and AIDs, the very effective self-help partnerships that have been developed can be offered practical administrative support and individuals and groups operating outside these networks can be linked into them. For women living with HIV this is the kind of work which is currently being done by organisations such as Womens Health Network as well as by individual nurses, social workers and volunteers.[6]

The work of detached youth workers with homeless young people, perhaps encouraging them to make use of drop-ins and other meeting places where they might gain access to mutual support as well as advice and information is also a good example of the way in which practical support can be combined with linking people into self-help networks.

Social work and self-advocacy

Increasingly, social workers are trying to find ways of working with networks of service users in order to promote self-advocacy (Croft and Beresford, 1989). But in doing so they need to learn from the experiences of others who have taken on the role of mediating between agency and community. Where the social worker is cast in the role of *broker* or *mediator* linking a community to a power structure with which the members of that community are in conflict, the role of self-help facilitator becomes highly problematic. A Muslim Asian community worker mediating between a local council and the local Asian community in trying to establish ethnically sensitive schooling was 'branded as an agitator by council officers and as in the pocket of councillors by some of the parents' (Ellis, 1989, p. 91).

Good work can be done even in circumstances like this but only if workers are able to negotiate a high level of autonomy for themselves and where agencies are able to to see their role as helpful to the eventual resolution of the conflict between agency and community.

Networking for empowerment

What follows is an account of networking to build communities of empowerment.

Enabling interpersonal relationships

In contrast to an earlier generation of radicals, a concern with interpersonal relationships is seen not as *victim blaming* but as an integral part of the process of empowering disadvantaged people.

As in any partnership people need to feel that the particulars of their own experience have been acknowledged. For self-helpers this often means recognising that although they may come together in relation to some issues, on other issues they may need to recognise a fundamental difference in the nature of their experience. Failure to do this is likely to lead to resentment and an inability to give even temporary priority to the issues which they do have in common.

As a male social work lecturer I have often seen groups of White female students attempt to create a shared sisterhood with Black female students. Unfortunately, in doing so, they are inclined to deny the difference between what it is to be a Black woman and what it is to be a White woman. Black female students, understandably tend to react angrily to this denial of their experience and respond by devaluing what they have in common in terms of gender with the White female students. They claim a priority for issues of race which the White female students feel unable to accept because this in turn feels like a denial of their experience. By this time both the Black and White female students are hurt, angry, and defensive and any hopes of sisterhood they might once have shared tend to fade away. Characteristically, while all this is going on, the power of White male students remains unchallenged.

Sometimes people can manage this process of accepting difference with little or no help from outsiders. Sometimes, however, they may need to be helped to do so. Those who feel marginalised need to be helped to stake a claim for acceptance. Whilst those who persist in seeing the *community* as a mirror image of themselves will need to be helped to see that to persist in this is likely to weaken rather than strengthen the community. In the case of the example, this would need someone — probably not a male lecturer — working separately with both Black and White students to bring them together to negotiate a new form of sisterhood.

Many communities gather around *community leaders* who act as brokers both within their emergent communities, and between these communities and those in positions of power and authority. These *leaders* can therefore exercise a profound influence for good or ill. It is vital that professionals trying to facilitate networks of empowerment have some strategy for addressing the role of *community leaders* which may mean providing opportunities for new *leaders* to come forward.

Ellis describes a situation in Rochdale in which a new Asian leadership emerges from a youth club to challenge the hold on power exerted by traditional community leaders based on mosques and the political parties (Ellis, 1989, p. 129).

Enabling community

If people do not identify with a *community* they will not participate in it. It is therefore vital that they have or are given the opportunity to talk to one another and thereby discover a sense of community.

A sense of community is often developed through social interaction and live experience rather than intellectual introspection. In some circumstances people may only identify with one another if they have already experienced each other as supportive. Grant and Wenger suggest that in the case of one carers' network a certain kind of supportive connectedness, which they call *interdependency* was needed to establish an awareness of network commonality. Working together in the same scheme for the care of elderly people, led to an *interdependency* among the helpers: frequent contact and consequent opportunities for helping one another (Grant & Wenger, 1983, pp. 45–47). This suggests that the fostering of *interdependency* may be seen as a networking strategy in its own right.

Helping a community to come together may sometimes mean helping it to diversify. Sometimes one community may not be enough. In relation to HIV, the impact of race, culture, and ethnicity may make it difficult for some people to get the support they need from the mainstream mainly White AIDS organisations. HIV positive Asian people, for example seem to be particularly isolated. In such situations social workers or other professionals, may have a role in catalysing the development of new forms of self-help amongst marginalised or minority groups. This can have the effect of enabling these groups to raise their issues with those who have claimed to speak for the whole community. Having done so, it may then be possible for all these groups to come together in a new, more diverse and mutually respectful partnership.

The distinctive feature about the *support* that a self-help network offers its members is that it is peer support, support to the disadvantaged from the disadvantaged. As oppression is a core experience, one which helps to structure an individual's sense of self, a link with others forged on the basis of a common oppression promotes a strong sense of collective identity which is easily translated into support. This property of self-help networks has been described as a 'new sociability built on situations and problems' (Bakker & Karel, 1983, p. 165). For professionals seeking to challenge oppression this *new sociability* may also be very important.

> White antiracist social workers need their own support networks to help them cope with their fears; and make demands which are impossible for individuals to take on alone, collectively (Dominelli 1988, p. 137).

Social support is particularly important when the commonality that binds a network together is experienced in a very personal and isolating manner. One of the 'aims and objectives' of the SHAKTI Network for South Asian lesbian and gay people is:

> To outreach into the Asian communities as a resource and link for those who find themselves lonely, isolated, insecure, afraid and persecuted because of their sexuality, from family, friends and their community (SHAKTI brochure).

In this way SHAKTI creates a *community* of the oppressed to replace other forms of more traditional *community* ruptured by the oppression against which that *community* will also campaign.

A *community* of this kind may be particularly important for people living with HIV. Moralistic attitudes and fear of contagion can lead to the effective loss of the informal network of family and friends. The result can be the *social and emotional alienation* of those who are known to have a positive diagnosis (Mantell et al 1989, p. 45). In situations like this, the community of interest can again function as a substitute for family and friends. Practical advice and help, emotional support, and general opportunities for socialising can all be obtained from a support network recruited from members of the positive community.

Unemployment may also be experienced in a very personal and isolating manner as it may undermine social networks. This may directly affect the health of unemployed people. Yet ironically, there is evidence that strong social networks can mitigate the impact of unemployment on the health of the unemployed person (Auslander, 1988, p. 197–98). One conclusion that can be drawn from this is that facilitating the growth of links between unemployed people might help to create a *community of the unemployed* with consequent benefits to their health (Auslander, 1988, pp. 198–99).

Relating to one another may also be very important for professionals. A number of women working in separate offices within the same Social Services Department might be feeling bad about themselves and their work. Perhaps looking simply for trouble sharing opportunities they might begin to meet up with one another. After a while commonalities may emerge in relation to part-time work; managing child care responsibilities; and working long and antisocial hours, etc. Gradually through discussion with one another, problems may be redefined and collective action undertaken, including campaigns within the Department and through the Union around issues such as child care vouchers, workplace nurseries, more flexible hours, etc.

Enabling flexibility and informality

One of the great strengths of self-help is its ability to operate free of the constraints which are inevitably imposed on those working for official bureaucracies. As Bakker and Karel writing of Dutch self-help note, this has enormous potential.

> Alongside the whole structure of existing official welfare and health facilities a new parallel infrastructure of self formed groups and support systems is showing up.....organised into new networks in order to promote various interests, independent of existing provisions (Bakker and Karel, 1983, p. 165).

But freedom to think and operate in new ways can be compromised if self-helpers feel they have to imitate the very bureaucracies with which they are so dissatisfied. This is a real danger, particularly in the UK where people seem to feel that they have to be properly constituted as a voluntary organisation complete with management committee, chairperson and minutes before they can do anything. This diverts energy from the key task of exploring the kind of partnership they might have with one another. It also tends to put off those for whom this way of doing things is very alien. For some, it may symbolise the conventional structures of power they are seeking to challenge.

By relating to one another in much more loosely structured ways, women, Black people, gay men and others have been able to involve more people in a wider range of activities than would have been the case if they had stuck to the conventional model of a voluntary organisation.

One of the main forces pushing self-help networks into becoming self-help organisations is the need for funding. This is often only forthcoming if the network has some kind of administrative structure. But even if realism dictates that the network takes this step, it does not automatically follow that it must abandon all its informal characteristics. This is not just a question of style it is also a question of accountability. If the organisation operates principally through its management committee and fails to consult regularly with all those who in a broader sense feel they own it, the result will be that the organisation will become alienated from its community.

Self-help networks exert a *pressure on the environment* (Bakker and Karel, 1983, p. 163). They force others and in particular official welfare agencies to respond to them. By refusing to play by the bureaucratic rules they are able to make the vital point that it is these rules which may well be part of the problem and they oblige welfare professionals to examine their own assumptions in ways which can lead to changes in the nature of *official welfare* services. But bureaucracies are very skilled at persuading people to fit into their view of the world and therefore self-helpers need to resist the temptation to be *good* — to adopt the role expected of them when in fact they are much more effective when they refuse to accept these roles.

The *voice* of the community will reflect the way it is structured. If it involves a wide range of people cooperating in an informal partnership that voice is not only likely to be more authentic, it is also more likely to avoid the danger of 'colonisation' by welfare bureaucracies, than if it has itself become a mini-bureaucracy.

Enabling communication

Self-help can be seen as an act of resistance — a challenge to both bureaucratic insensitivity and institutionalised discrimination. A vital aspect of this is the promotion of new and positive imagery. This is not only relevant for campaigning. It also represents the *feel good* factor of empowerment and enables oppressed people to build a *culture of resistance* or a way of perceiving themselves and the world which is embued with this positive imagery.

The social model of disability, black consciousness, and feminism can all be seen not only as theories of oppression but as attempts to create an alternative language and set of values by which to live. This is not easy to accomplish. But only relatively close-knit social networks are able to generate their own values and norms (Bott, 1971, p. 60). When these values and norms are diametrically opposed to the dominant views in society, it may be even more essential that those involved are in close contact with one another.

From one point of view, the ideal communication network for a *community of interest* involves a relatively small number of people all of whom are in constant touch with one another. This allows the members of the network to build up their own culture; to reinforce one another's confidence; and challenge the oppressive views of outsiders. Localised campaigns and support groups can build on these advantages to good effect. But any self-help network is likely to be more effective if it is able to operate also at a national or international level. Some issues can only be dealt with at these levels where it is essential that relatively large numbers of people are involved. There appears to be an inverse relationship between what is needed for individuals to feel strong and confident and what is needed to be really effective at anything other than a very local level. This is a significant paradox which self-helpers need to resolve.

One solution to this communications' paradox is to make use of meetings and newsletters both of which *boost* the level of communication. Meetings enable those who participate to reinforce their sense of community identity by sharing information and interpretations of events which serve to confirm their collective values, their ways of identifying themselves, and their sense of participating in a common struggle. Very often, these strategies can be combined with very positive results.

The Images network of groups involved in work with young women in Cumbria arose out of the recognition that a number of people were working with the same issues in similar ways but in places too distant to allow for informal face-to-face contact. Given the way work with young girls is frequently marginalised by the dominant youth work culture which tends to focus on boys and their needs, some opportunity to interact with and support one another was clearly a priority. A cheese and wine party attended by people from all over Cumbria led on to the founding of a newsletter *Images* which seems to have been very successful in developing a community identity (Youth Club, 1989).

Whilst specific issues can help to draw together a large number of people, maintaining a communication network when there is no specific issue to work on usually requires some deliberate action.

> Within London antiracist activists have found programmes of meetings on a citywide basis maintain a Londonwide communication network through which campaign issues can be spotted at an early stage enabling the communication network to be expanded into a campaign when appropriate.[7]

But not everyone likes going to meetings and not everyone reads newsletters. One of the commonest mistakes made by those who enjoy these things is to ignore the bulk of people who do not. This is almost bound to lead to a rather inward looking tendency perhaps accompanied by a preoccupation with ideological purity and the consequent uprooting of heresy. This is, for example the fate that seems to have befallen most small left-wing political parties. A key issue then is the creation and maintenance of a communication network linking activists and others. In the above example of an antiracist network, the role of the activists who meet with one another should then be to inform others who are sympathetic and might participate at some future date in antiracist actions around London. The model therefore would be of a core network of activists interacting closely with one another but linked individually as *brokers* to a wide range of other people.

Enabling action-sets

A *self-help network* is an *action-set*. It can be mobilised either on behalf of one of its members or collectively in pursuit of common interests. The mutual support that community members give one another has been described already. Here we will be concerned with the active pursuit of collective *interests* — campaigning.

Some of the most successful antiracist campaigns have focused on specific issues such as the link between racism and homelessness in London. This involved *headline grabbing* actions such as the occupation of a town hall in protest at the number of Black families living in bed and breakfast hotels.[8]

But not all campaigns need to be so dramatic. Some of the most effective campaigns are the result of undramatic but consistent pressure.

Effecting a general shift in opinion in society has been called a *silent mobilisation* (Bakker & Karel, 1983, p. 162) — a process of striving for an acceptance of:

different definition of the position of the individual client or patient — for instance, by fighting for better legal status, the right to complain or participation in the treatment process (Bakker & Karrel, 1983, p. 166).

In the UK a loose network of children presently and formerly in the care of local authorities, spearheaded by the National Association for Young People in Care, through their continuous protests achieved an effective *silent mobilisation* by gradually convincing most child care professionals that children in care should have a right to be present at and participate in important meetings deciding their future (Stein and Ellis, 1983).

Sometimes the educational activity of a radical network can be more clearly targeted and specific than is implied by a *silent mobilisation.* The *disabled civil rights movement* in the USA operated very effectively as a lobbying network to create the political conditions for the passage of the 1989 *Americans with Disabilities Act.* This lobbying power reflected the increasing growth of a nationwide network of disabled people: the product of a purposeful empowering strategy.

> Even five years ago there wasn't this type of networking. We're making real strides now', said Elizabeth Lilley, a networking activist recently' (Dourado, 1990, p. 17).

It is impossible to draw a hard and fast distinction between what is needed to put together a campaign and what is needed to develop a more general sense of community. Issues of mutual support, an ability to participate fully in decision making processes; acceptance and a sense of mutual identification have to be considered whenever a campaign is to be mounted.

In relation to feminist social work it has been pointed out that

> the identity of campaigns can also be indissoluble from their existence as networks ministering to individual women (Dominelli & McLeod, 1989, p. 46).

A good example of this within Social Services Departments are networks of female social workers who have in common experiences of sexual abuse disclosure work. Network members often offer each other personal support in coping with and making sense of the complicated, painful and angry feelings raised by the work itself and its impact on relations with male colleagues and even partners. In addition, these networks may also *campaign* within their Departments to ensure that feminist perspectives are included in training courses, male managers are sensitised to the issues, etc.

Campaigning always rests on a collective understanding of the resources within a network; an ability to mobilise those resources; and a collective willingness to take the risk of doing something. Much also depends on the presence or absence of *animateurs*, people who can make things happen. These may not be established *community leaders* and indeed the challenge of organising a campaign may facilitate the emergence of new *animateurs*.

Cooperation or conflict?

Increasingly powerful criticisms are being made of the way in which *communities of interest* can all too easily come into conflict with one another. In the context of social work education, this has been described as the *proliferation of the isms* (Cooper and Pitts, 1989, p. 17). For voluntary organisations based upon *communities of interest* this process may become particularly acute when the *isms* compete with one another for financial support, or even when organisations associated with and attempting to represent different ethnic *communities* bid against one another for local authority grants setting back any attempt to build a broader antiracist community[9]. Also, for the dubious advantage of occupying the topmost rung in the hierarchy of oppression, oppressed groups may use up more energy attacking each other than on developing solidarity with one another. As awareness of the subtleties of oppression grows, new *communities of interest* are born and new fragmentations and conflicts may arise.

Whilst members of a *community of interest* are often very successful in finding ways of communicating with each other, there is always a danger of being too inward looking. This reflects the tendency to define the *community* in opposition to other *communities*. The challenge for networking is to establish links between *communities of interest* to open up debate and discussion, and perhaps even the possibility of alliance around new commonalities. One way of creating new alliances has been pioneered by resource centres which provide opportunities for various *communities of interest* to network between themselves.

> People who use the centre meet each other and without any other intervention, horizons can be widened, prejudices weakened, and people can get new ideas. Trade union groups find out what tenants' groups are doing,... women from a playgroup discover they have more in common with a local women's group than they thought... (Taylor, 1983, p. 22).

Summary

Empowerment begins with overcoming the fundamental oppression of isolation. Out of this process new *communities of interest* emerge all the time. Because all these *communities* involve a wide range of different people who could choose to identify themselves in very different ways, these *communities* are also partnerships with the following characteristics:

1. Self-help partnerships have to acknowledge difference as well as commonality. All those involved need to feel that their issues are being acknowledged. Some individuals are likely to take on key roles in *brokering* any self-help network. As part of this mediating role they may need to help different groups within the network to accept one another. Professionals can help to link individuals to existing networks and facilitate the processes by which self-helpers reach out to and come to terms with one another.

2. Self-help partnerships can forge new community identities and feelings. One aspect of this is that people realise that they are not alone with their problems. Coming together may be an opportunity to redefine personal issues as fundamentally political. As oppression is very isolating, one benefit of self-help may well be the creation of a support network which can substitute for other *lost* communities. Professionals can facilitate these community processes in a number of practical ways, eg by helping people to find a place where they can meet.

3. Self-help is informal. Self-helpers do not necessarily have to constitute themselves as formal organisations. Often they might be well advised not to, at least in the early stages. The ability to take on a variety of roles in relation to one another is one of the strengths of self-help. Moreover, they should avoid being *colonised* by welfare agencies who may wish to impose their own oppressive expectations on self-help partnerships. Professionals can help by themselves avoiding the temptation to *colonise* and, more positively, by strengthening self-helpers in their resolve to go their own way.

4. Self-help partnerships depend on empowering forms of communication. An effective communication network can facilitate the development of a new *language* through which positive self-images can be promoted. A large network may experience communication difficulties. Meetings can enhance face-to-face contact: newsletters can also help. But, it is important that activists do not only talk to one another — professionals may be able to advise about communication possibilities and provide some practical help eg with newsletters.

5. Self-help partnerships are action oriented partnerships. Self-helpers form *action-sets* around one another for mutual support. They form *campaigns* with one another to fight for social change. Campaigning can be short-term and specific, or long-term and more oriented to changing values, attitudes and practices.

Communities can come into conflict with one another. They are less likely to do so if their members perceive that they can form partnerships with one another for their mutual benefit. Social workers and other professionals may be able to contribute to this process.

8 Networkers as community brokers

Networking skills

Networking is concerned with enabling community partnerships to grow and sustain themselves. There are many different kinds of community partnership: There are those in neighbourhoods and those between agencies. Some are set up for therapeutic purposes and others developed as a result of case management. There are also those community partnerships which people build to empower themselves. As a result, we cannot point to one activity and say, 'that is what networking is all about'.

At first sight, this seems to suggest that we cannot say anything very useful about networking skills. Either we sum them up in a few bland generalisations, or we decide there are as many skills as there are examples of community partnership and proceed to list them. If we choose the first option we are reduced to comments such as 'networkers need to know how to relate to other people' which are so general as to be meaningless. If we choose the second option we are likely to give up in boredom or exhaustion before we ever reach the end of our list of skills.

But this position is reached with a persistent search for a unique and distinctive set of networking techniques. They do not exist [10]. If we define skills as techniques, it is apparent that those involved in networking are not new. Anyone starting to network will be able to draw on techniques that either they already possess, or could learn doing something else. Moreover networking is eclectic and so, at any one time, may involve using techniques developed by group workers, community workers, case workers and others. What is different about networking is not the techniques themselves but the way that they are combined with one another and the purposes to which they are applied. This is where the real skills lie and any discussion of networking skills has to take place in the context of a discussion about the role of the networker.

Community brokers

Whatever the context, networkers act as brokers: brokers of people; brokers of information; and brokers of resources (Mayer, 1966, p. 109). This involves a number of complementary sub-roles, two of which are illustrated with reference to a very basic networking situation — the three cornered relationship between an isolated elderly person, a neighbourhood care organiser and a social worker.

Mr Shah is eighty years old. His wife died several years ago. They had no children. After retiring he lost contact with his colleagues at work, became rather depressed and more and more reclusive. A referral is received from his neighbour, who does not want to be directly involved herself but feels concerned about him. The social worker visits and discovers that Mr Shah would welcome a visit from one of the local members of a *good neighbours* scheme, many of whom are Asian. A referral is made to the organiser of the scheme who visits, finds someone whom she feels Mr Shah would relate to well and both the social worker and the scheme organiser introduce this person to Mr Shah. Their relationship is a little tense and formal at first but after some initial miscommunication and misunderstanding, Mr Shah begins to value his regular contacts with the *good neighbour*. The relationship blossoms and they even go out of the house together on several occasions.

Told in this way, it does not seem as if the social worker has been particularly skilful. It appears to be a relatively straightforward piece of work which does not make any great demands on the social worker involved. But all is not as it seems.

There is much that could have gone wrong: the organiser might have wondered why a social worker should want to refer Mr Shah. Was he so difficult that the social worker could not cope with him any more? From her point of view, other social workers had made inappropriate referrals in the past, just to save themselves work. Why should this be any different? The initial misunderstandings between Mr Shah and his visitor could have drawn the organiser and the social worker into conflict with one another. The social worker might have felt that the visitor should only engage in general chit-chat and leave any *counselling* to professionals. When Mr Shah and the visitor began to discuss more *personal* issues, the social worker might have become anxious about his or her role and sought to place (unwelcome) restrictions on the activities of the visitor.

What is remarkable in this case is that none of these things have happened or if they have happened they have been worked through with little difficulty. It can therefore help us to begin to analyse some aspects of the role of *community broker*.

Community brokers invest in key relationships

In this case the key figure was the organiser of the good neighbours scheme. Long before anything was known about Mr Shah,

the social worker had realised that it was very important to ensure that there should be mutual understanding and mutual
respect in their dealings with one another and had started a
programme of regular liaison meetings to discuss issues such as
how referrals should be made. The joint introduction by the
social worker and the organiser of the visitor to Mr Shah was part
of a package of *good practice* measures agreed at these liaison
meetings.

Relationships between networkers and certain key individuals
can make or break a partnership. These have to be nurtured and
networkers often need to work hard to establish trust and credibility. Key figures may be a service user, an influential neighbourhood figure; a person working for another agency; a relative or a
friend; sometimes another sort of person altogether. In all cases
however, the person is key because he or she is in a position to
either deliver a community partnership or to destroy or disable it.
One way of thinking about this is that networkers need to know
the identity of those who *gatekeep* community resources and as
community brokers they need to invest in building the kind of
relationships with them which will allow information and resources to flow freely to where they are needed.

Community brokers handle conflicts by raising awareness

> Mr Shah and his visitor experience some difficulties in their relation-
> ship and Mr Shah complains to the social worker and the visitor
> complains to the organiser. The social worker, however realises that
> it is more important to explore what is going on rather than to
> blame other people because something has gone wrong. Acting as a
> *community broker* the social worker talks to all concerned and helps
> them to talk to one another about what has happened. In conse-
> quence, there is a collective realisation that Mr Shah does not want
> the visitor to come without an appointment. He wants to keep a
> *special* time for the visit and sees this as a way of valuing it. The
> visitor interpreted this as unfriendliness. When the organiser realised
> that Mr Shah was not asking for anything more than an element of
> predictability, she was able to help the visitor to see the issue in
> practical terms as simply a question of how times for visits were to
> be arranged in advance.

Generally, every pattern of interaction has its own properties and
as community brokers, networkers help people to focus on the
specificities of their relationships in order to improve the

effectiveness of their partnership with one another. As in this example it is not a question of imposing anything but rather of helping people to become aware of the pattern of their relationships. If this pattern is problematic, ways in which they could work together to change it can be identified. This is as true of a pattern of family relationships as it is of a pattern of inter-agency relationships.

Community brokers are change-agents

Although we could discuss the issue of change in relation to the original example, it might be better to do so in relation to some rather more complex and crisis laden situation.

> Henrietta Plowden is a woman of eighty-four. She lives alone. She has Alzheimer's disease and will not allow anyone except her daughter-in-law to shop, clean or cook for her. A network conference is called to respond to an imminent crisis arising from the fact that the daughter-in-law is shortly due to go on holiday for two weeks.
>
> The case manager who chairs the conference realises that this problem may be an opportunity to renegotiate the pattern of network partnership. The support network could be redesigned engaging the daughter-in-law with other, presently, more peripherally involved people such as a home help, a volunteer visitor, and the warden of the sheltered housing scheme where the client lives. The case manager's aim is to solve both the immediate problem and the longer term problems related to an over concentration of care in one part of the network by facilitating the development of a more effective *interwoven* network. In other words, the case manager spots the opportunity for change and takes it.

But having a strategy and seizing an opportunity are not enough. There also needs to be a clear plan of action:

> The daughter-in-law could be accompanied by the home help — whom the client normally only allows to make a cup of tea — on several visits to her mother-in-law prior to going on holiday. By sharing tasks with the daughter-in-law on these visits the home help might be accepted as a substitute by the client in the daughter-in-law's absence. On her return, the daughter-in-law could be careful not to resume all her previous tasks, but only some of them. If successful a similar procedure could be used to introduce other under-used helpers to more significant roles in the life of the client

Major change often involves attention to detail and network change is no exception to this principle. But however strong the case for change, it can be overwhelming (Toffler 1971, pp. 11–26). Here we can see that the case manager not only works towards change but anticipates resistance to change both from Ms. Plowden and perhaps less obviously, from other members of the caring network and takes account of it in the action plan. Although Ms. Plowden, her daughter-in-law and the home help are all being asked to make changes in how they relate to one another, nobody is being asked to make so many changes that they are likely to feel they have lost control of the pace of change. Moreover, the fact that the action plan is agreed at a network conference means that all those involved contract for change with one another. This provides the mandate for change.

But not everything can be forseen. As a community broker, networkers have to be responsive to signals that not everyone is happy with changes which may have been made.

A child protection conference might become alarmed by a deterioration in the quality of care being given to a child and suggest that a family aide involved with the family should explain to the parents that she would be focusing much more on surveillance and much less on general befriending than in the past. This might be justified but if the family aide did not realise that she might be expected to undertake this kind of work, she might refuse to implement the conference decision. In situations like this, it is always important to recognise that individuals may have their own very strong views about the nature of their contract with the rest of the network and that recontracting is likely to be more productive than insisting their views are wrong.

Networkers need to be aware of unplanned as well as planned change and to be able to respond to the pattern of events as they emerge. New and unforeseen problems may emerge as a consequence of implementing networking strategies which may undermine the work if they are not attended to promptly.

Encouraging a small number of younger disabled people to forge stronger links with a larger number of older disabled people living near each other to meet more regularly with them, to engage in more shared social activities and a campaign directed towards common mobility issues might lead to the younger disabled people feeling that their needs and concerns were being swallowed up by the needs and concerns of the older majority. There may be a need to mix joint activities with some separate activities.

Finally in relation to the management of change, it needs to be recognised that the development of a community partnership involves the evolution of a new culture for participants. Moreover it is likely to be a culture of innovation, risk taking and self-evaluation. On the last point, it is clear that certain kinds of networks can provide enormous opportunities for mutual learning — a community partnership can be seen as one of these *action learning sets* (Gay, 1983). But all this can be very stressful and networkers need to find ways of supporting people through this process of cultural transformation.

Community brokers are holistic

The process of linking individuals, groups or organisations with one another requires that everything is taken into account: not just the immediate goals of the partnership.

> For example, it might seem to a number of professionals that all those agencies involved in child sexual abuse work in a particular area might benefit from linking together in a multidisciplinary *team.* As a result a new network might be formed consisting of police, paediatricians, psychologists and social workers. However, it may quickly emerge that all the members of this *team* were approaching their work with different priorities and even different values.

Until issues of confidentiality, criminal investigation, treatment, punishment, and a range of other issues were resolved, this team would be unable to function. If the concept of the multidisciplinary *team* had been planned more accurately, awareness of these issues might have led instead, to an initial set of more general inter-agency liaisons. Familiarising agencies with one another's practices including inter-agency meetings could resolve barriers to effective partnership. After these preliminary forms of brokerage had been established the agency network would be able to move towards inter-disciplinary *teams.*

Community brokers are interpreters

Those who speak different languages sometimes need an interpreter in order to communicate. But it is not just differences of language which sometimes lead to mutual incomprehension. Whenever we attempt to reach out to others who may not see the world in our way we may simply fail to understand one another. And yet, we cannot make links with others unless we understand something about them. It is always much easier to stereotype or caricature other people than it is to make the effort to understand practices which may, at first, appear strange or mystifying. But unless someone takes the risk of trying to comprehend and then to help others to understand it will not be possible for a community partnership to be built. This is as true of inter-agency relationships as it is of personal relationships.

There are several stages involved in the process of inter-agency interpreting.

The first stage is what one could call the *ethnographic* stage in which the emphasis is on simply meeting with and talking to potential partners and trying to build up a sense of how they see their work and what their priorities might be in any partnership with your own agency.

The second stage is what one could call the *lingua franca* stage in which the broker helps the agencies to understand one another.

We can apply this to the relations between local authority social work teams and small voluntary organisations. These are often difficult because contacts are too superficial to promote a real understanding of each other's work. Moreover these difficulties may prevent a proper evaluation of each other's strengths. For more collaboration between the voluntary and the statutory sectors of care in the future, more effort needs to be made by them to develop an understanding of one another's work.

The interpretive approach outlined above might reveal to a statutory social work team that the lack of clear policy or line management accountability complained of by them in relation to a small voluntary organisation might give that organisation a flexibility and willingness to experiment. This could be invaluable in setting up imaginative *packages of care*. At the same time the small voluntary organisation might discover that the *bureaucracy* of the statutory social work team is associated with a capacity to deliver reliable and predictable services on a long term basis that they are unable to match.

Community brokers are power sharers

One of the dangers of brokerage is that it can lead to an accumulation of power in the hands of the *broker*. In a political context, this may be one of the main reasons why people act as *brokers* (Mayer, 1969, pp. 113–14). However, in a social work context, any unnecessary accumulation of power by professionals is counter productive. It is certainly unlikely to facilitate the empowerment of clients who may have a 'history of powerlessness and enforced passivity' (Rose, and Black, 1985, p. 82). An essential brokerage skill is therefore the ability to counteract this tendency by using one's own position as an intermediary to open up channels of communication for others rather than to continue to monopolise communication.

Inter-agency liaisons which are conducted on a one-to-one basis have a potential to exclude other members of the organisations involved from participation. Combining regular one-to-one communication with occasional larger scale meetings between a range of agency representatives can be helpful in preventing *broker* monopolisation of the liaisons developing.

At the inter-agency level, the broker agency should see its liaisons as an opportunity to introduce other agencies to one another rather than seeking to channel all inter-agency communication through itself. Fundamentally, there is a need to develop the attitude that brokerage is about opening up contact and communication.

When trying to build networks of support around individual service users, the issue of power is even more crucial. For example, as has already been demonstrated, case managers may inadvertently oppress both service users and carers if they monopolise channels of communication and fail to enable people to build their own patterns of *connectedness* with one another (*see* Chapter 6).

Community broker as systems broker

Networking tends to create chains of practice within which community partnerships are linked to and supportive of one another. One way of thinking about this is that the chain of practice grows as the individual networker progressively facilitates the growth of new partnerships which all support one another and all address different aspects of the same situation. Let us look first at this type of systems brokerage.

Chain of practice

> A local health visitor and a patch social worker might work with each other on complex child care cases concerning a number of homeless families temporarily living within the patch. Although, they find that they often approach their work in a different way they value each other's contributions and begin to explore the possibility of an inter-agency liaison to promote collaborative work. When they discuss this idea with their managers, they get a positive response. But it seems also that as the major shared concern would be homeless families, the liaison should cover all those health visitors and social workers who work with this client group, many of whom live outside the boundaries of the original patch.

Eventually a number of local liaisons are started but all those involved also meet as a *special interest group* on a regular basis. Members of this special interest group then begin to work together on projects, one of which is the development of new creche/playgroup facilities in some of the hotels and hostels being used to house homeless families. This project meets with an enthusiastic response from some homeless families who involve themselves in it and initiate their own campaign. This gradually expands to encompass all the issues facing them as a consequence of living in temporary accommodation.

The process of building a set of partnerships can be seen as a process of discovery, in which the links between issues are revealed with personal and political strategies combined. A whole range of feedback possibilities arise, through which the issues dealt with by one partnership can inform the work done by another. In this example, the health visitor and social worker may well encourage individual clients to participate in the playspace campaign or in general campaigns about homelessness whilst, at the same time cooperating closely in their more individualised supportive work.

Partnership system

Chains of practice are one form of systems brokerage in which a network of interrelated partnerships is created as a result of a single chain of events. More often, however, a number of events and a number of different individuals and organisations may contribute to the development of such a network.

A *network of partnerships* is a partnership system. If the overall system is to be effective, it is vital that all those involved have some awareness of their relationship to it. This means that the partnership system as a whole needs to be brokered. Brokering should ensure that the parts facilitate the whole and the whole facilitates the parts.

Making certain that the partnership system works is becoming increasingly important as social policy puts an increasing emphasis on communication, cooperation and collaboration between professionals, service users, families and others. This emphasis is revolutionising services for both adults and children. It is clear that services to *children in need* and their families will entail effective inter-agency collaboration, for example between Housing and Social Services Departments and between different local authorities. The issues are even clearer in relation to services for adults.

Community care—a case for systems brokerage

The case management/care management system which is the centrepiece of the government's community care policy, cannot exist in isolation. The case management partnership needs to be supported by a complex partnership system. To some extent the need for 'a fully integrated system which is geared to the support of the care management process' is already recognised (DOH, SSI, 1991a, p. 66). But whilst it has been acknowledged that community care is not yet a 'seamless service' (DOH, SSI, 1991b, p. 21), it has not yet been fully appreciated that the process of integrating *information systems, service planning, service contracting, quality assurance, service monitoring, management support* and *training* (DOH, SSI. 1991a, p. 66) cannot be separated from general issues of coordination and collaboration. In other words, we need to see the community care system, as a whole, as a partnership system.

1. Those involved in planning accessible information services will need to be involved in discussions with libraries, advice centres, health centres and other community facilities. They will also need to have links with social workers and others involved with service users, carers and their representatives and self-advocacy groups. They will also need to feedback to all those involved with service delivery as to whether the information which is provided is adequate or indeed whether it seriously misrepresents the reality of what is on offer!

2. The choices available to service users and their carers will be dependent upon the ability of agencies to collaborate with one another on service development. Developments will be ineffective unless they address in a relevant way the needs which are uncovered through the case management/care management process. Developmental units will thus need good links with case/care managers, service providers, and service users/carers.

3. Developmental work will need to feed into service contracting arrangements and if, as seems likely, *service menus* are put together not by individual case/care managers but by others, the links between these three divisions will be of great significance.

4. All parts of the community care system need to be *quality assured.* This means that the criteria set for specific bits of the system need to complement one another. There needs to be a way of ensuring that those involved in all parts of the system feedback to one another. Therefore service monitoring cannot just consist of specific input/output measures (DOH, SSI, 1991a pp. 69–70). It also has to consist of ways of evaluating the part played by the service in the overall community care system. This can only be done if information is shared and discussions are opened up through a quality assurance partnership.

5. Management support cannot just mean the direct support of workers. Managers should liaise with their opposite numbers in other units, divisions, or agencies and simultaneously build supportive structures for their own workers.
6. Training has to draw upon the experience of case/managers, service providers, service users and their carers and has to be linked to the processes of service development in order to ensure that it is relevant and useful.

Increasingly, all those involved with the development of community care will have to look towards models of partnership in order to develop 'plural yet integrated, systems of care management' (DOH, SSI, 1991a p. 74).

Brokering the community care system

There has been an increasing recognition that the development of a *seamless* community care service will depend in large part on the effectiveness of *lead managers* (DOH, SSI, 1991b, p. 22). But to really grasp partnership opportunities these *lead managers* should be allowed to operate not just as inter-agency negotiators but as brokers facilitating and coordinating a number of wide ranging partnerships between service users, carers, professionals and agencies to create the kind of culture within which case management and service delivery can be effective.

Community care is not unique. We need to recognise that partnership systems of all kinds will grow in importance in future years. As they do so they will raise questions of coordination and integration which can only be addressed if there are specific individuals enabled to conceive their role in networking terms. This raises interesting questions not just about community care but also about the whole nature of management in the new social services' world. If managers are to be networkers this suggests that the key management task may increasingly be the management of the negotiating process.

Summary

Networking shamelessly borrows techniques from all branches of social and community work. Its real skills lie in handling a role, that of *community broker*. As community brokers, networkers develop the links or spin the web of community and this involves a number of characteristic activities.

1. Community brokers access community partnerships by working with and through key individuals. They have to take a long-term view and be prepared to invest in those relationships.
2. Community brokers are untanglers of *knotty* relationships. They try to resolve unhelpful conflicts by promoting a shared awareness of the way in which people relate to one another.
3. Community brokers are promoters and managers of change. This involves:
   a. strategic thinking;
   b. opportunism;
   c. developing action plans;
   d. working with and planning for resistance to change;
   e. helping people to accept cultural change.
4. Community brokers are systemic in their approach. They are concerned with developing patterns of partnership which take account of all aspects of the partnership situation, especially possible sources of conflict and misunderstanding.
5. Community brokers work towards mutual understanding. They need to have a capacity to see things from the other person's point of view. They use this understanding to help those who might otherwise be quite uncomprehending of one another to find ways of communicating and working with one another.
6. Community brokers use their mediating position to raise the level of contact and communication between partnership members. They do not seek to increase their own power by monopolising channels of communication.

The concept of the *community broker* can also be extended to the process by which *networkers* develop links between a number of interrelated community partnerships. Because this is brokerage at the level of the partnership system we can call this *systems brokerage*. It can develop organically, with networkers setting up different types of *community partnership* one after another as they recognise that certain problems need to be tackled at several different levels simultaneously. It can also develop in a more piecemeal fashion as a wide range of people work towards an integrated approach to a particular issue. Community care is a good example of a vision which is likely to become a reality only through some form of *systems brokerage*.

9 Community assessment: a networking approach

Community assessment

The concept of a *community assessment* is not new. For many years it has been recognised that we cannot make an assessment even of individual needs without taking account of the broad social context in which people live which helps to shape the pattern of those needs. But these *community assessments* whether undertaken by social workers, community workers or nurses (Reinhardt and Quinn, 1973, pp. 174–75) tend to focus on background factors or broad profiles of need which is often difficult to relate to specific situations. In contrast the networking approach to *community assessment* always starts with a specific situation which is analysed in network terms. This analysis may be informed by awareness of the general social context but pictures individuals as active makers of their social worlds rather than helpless victims.

Another characteristic feature of the networking approach to assessment is that it is not something which is done to others but something which is always undertaken in partnership with others. In other words, for networkers, the partnership principle is as much a feature of the process of assessment as it is of the goals of assessment. This does not mean that networkers do not formulate their own ideas about situations. It means that they are always prepared to negotiate about them.

This chapter attempts to answer some of the questions raised by an assessment practice based on network and partnership principles.

How do networkers discover needs?

As social workers we inherit a tradition which goes back to the Victorian Poor Law of waiting for people to come to us on the assumption that they will do so if they really need help. However, if we are interested in offering a preventative service which does not undermine the citizenship of those who come to us for help, we have to be concerned with developing non-stigmatising channels by which people can communicate their needs. The networking response emphasises the role communication networks can play as non-stigmatising channels linking networkers to those who might be best placed to transmit information about need.

It takes time to develop an effective communication network but we have to be prepared to take a long-term perspective on this and invest in key relationships. We should not be asking ourselves how we pick up specific bits of information. Rather, we should be developing the kinds of relationships and communication networks that will enable people to communicate with us about their needs.

For this purpose, professionals need community contacts and some contacts will be more useful than others. The specific question which social workers or other professionals always need to address is: who are the *gatekeepers?* Who are the people who are likely to simultaneously give access to needs and the elements of a community partnership? The answer will, of course, depend on the situation.

Home helps who live in the area in which they also work are often useful mediators between Social Services Departments and local residents. I was involved in developing home help/social worker liaison projects in two different local authorities which attempted to provide a context in which social workers could relate to home helps as key neighbourhood figures. Social workers made themselves available when home helps came to the office developing a network of contacts with them.

Like all the most effective communication systems this one was based on information exchange. Social workers gave advice and information about social security benefits, sheltered housing and other *practical* issues. They also offered consultation and support with more complex and stressful situations. Home helps for their part alerted social workers to particular issues and problems. Slowly but surely, and without having, at first to do more than meet with home helps the social workers involved in the liaison were able to become part of the neighbourhood communication network linking the home helps to a large number of vulnerable people and those involved with supporting them.

Probably because home helps themselves felt helped, they were able to work more effectively. It also seems as if every act of help whether direct or indirect deepened and strengthened relationships. This communication network could be seen as a *virtuous circle* in which positive responses to those needs which were presented made it more likely that information about other needs would be transmitted.

Generally, the most effective way of discovering the needs
which a partnership should address, is to focus initially on the
needs of those who are in a position to deliver a community
partnership. By responding positively to their needs, networkers
create the channels of communication along which subsequent
messages about a range of other needs will be transmitted.

Sometimes the gatekeeper will be a carer; sometimes another
professional; sometimes there will be more than one gatekeeper.
But across a whole range of situations from inter-agency work to
case management, it seems as if assessment is dependent upon an
ability to negotiate with community *gatekeepers*.

How do we negotiate a communication network?

Community gatekeepers are *brokers*. One broker may lead to
another, who may in turn introduce the network to the rest of the
network. For example, it is quite possible that a home help may
communicate a concern to a social worker through a pre-existing
liaison link of the kind described above.

Joan Nicholson is a frail and mentally confused older woman. The
home help introduces the social worker to a key *informal* carer, Ms
Nicholson's neighbour, but cannot introduce the social worker to
any of the other people who are involved in supporting her in her
own home. The neighbour may be the only member of the informal
caring network with whom the home help is in direct contact. The
neighbour has acted as a representative of the informal caring network and the other carers may have been quite happy that all their
communications with the home help should have gone through her.
Up until now the neighbour and the home help, may, between each
other, have successfully managed the interface between the *formal*
and *informal* parts of the caring network.

Having made contact with the community gatekeepers and with
Joan Nicholson, the social worker realises that there is already a
community partnership in existence but that it is no longer able to
cope with the situation. If all those involved are to be helped to find
new ways of coping, then the social worker needs to talk to everyone and not just the neighbour and the home help. This will have to
be done without undermining them as they will continue to play
key caring roles.

A number of different networking strategies might work. What
follows is one possible strategy for opening up communication
possibilities whilst respecting the position of the two community
gatekeepers.

1. Meet with the neighbour, the home help and Joan Nicholson to define the issues as they see them. Establish the neighbour and the home help as key players in the community partnership and find out who else is involved.
2. Arrange to visit other members of the informal caring network with the neighbour or through introductions effected by the neighbour. Involve the home help in these meetings, if possible.
3. Arrange subsequent meetings with these other people without the presence of the neighbour if there are indications of conflicting views about the situation.
4. Arrange a network conference to enable all information to be shared and a new partnership to be established.

But no strategy can guarantee that fundamental conflicts of views or values may not emerge nor that communication may not become blocked, perhaps because of the existence of these conflicts.

Can there be an assessment if some of the partners are in conflict with one another?

An elderly woman living alone was gradually withdrawing from responsibility for her own life. I felt, rightly or wrongly that those involved with her had to do everything possible to reverse this process. Another social worker involved in the assessment partnership disagreed with me vehemently, feeling, rightly or wrongly, that decline was irreversible and that we should collectively assume responsibility for the client's welfare.

Because neither of us was in a position to impose our views on others involved in the situation and because we were both committed to the partnership, we were both exposed to pressure from other members of the partnership to compromise and explore the middle ground. The partnership not only survived the conflict but ensured that the assessment and planning process was undertaken from a much more realistic perspective than would have been possible if either I or the other social worker had had sole responsibility for the assessment.

A different situation arises when someone outside the context of the existing assessment partnership intervenes to block its work. When this happens, we need to follow the trail of resistance back to its source and reorientate the framework of assessment to take account of this resistance.

An attempt by social workers to liaise with district nurses or health visitors to explore joint staffing of *family advice sessions* at a local community centre may initially meet with an enthusiastic response, but as some of the implications begin to emerge, the health workers may become much less enthusiastic. Communication becomes increasingly awkward and meetings less productive. It turns out that a number of senior managers are not happy about the project and are effectively blocking it. The nurses and health visitors will therefore not be able to participate in the assessment exercise unless *permission* from their seniors is granted.

Communication will continue to be muffled unless the social workers and their managers succeed in negotiating *permission* for discussions to continue with the relevant health service managers. This *permission* might only be granted on certain conditions, one of which might be that they themselves would be involved in some of the meetings. This would, in fact, be very helpful, because then it would be possible to openly discuss any concerns they might have without these concerns acting as a general block on communication.

This shows the importance of ensuring that the assessment partnership includes all those who might have an interest in its work and the power to either facilitate or to disable it.

Sometimes, assessment may be blocked not because there are powerful individuals preventing others from speaking out but because some people feel they cannot express their true feelings or their real needs. This kind of self-censorship is in effect a withdrawal from partnership and may seriously distort the assessment process. To deal with situations like this, a social worker will need to attend to *implicit*, as well as *explicit* messages.

Many carers may feel that they have little choice but to care for aged and infirm parents, spouses and children. When asked directly they might well say that they want to continue caring for their dependent relative.

But anyone seeking to put together an appropriate *care package* in such a situation who simply took this at face value and did not pay attention to *process* clues such as tiredness, frustration, anger or depression would be likely to miss an important part of the message, that part which says 'I feel exhausted, trapped, devalued and unhelped by everyone, including you'! Messages like this are silenced because they are in conflict with assumptions about how carers ought to feel in our *patriarchal* society (Gittins, 1985, p. 131). This has been reflected in the way professionals have until recently ignored the needs of carers (Hicks, 1988)

But knowing how to open up communication or how to over-come blocks on communication will not be of any use if we do not know who or what we are communicating about.

Who is the client?

Whilst, it is not true that networking has little or no interest in the individual, it is true to say that for networkers, the individual is always part of a social field of some kind. This suggests that for networkers the client is a social field. But, this would be a false conclusion to draw. To clarify this issue, we need to go back to basics and ask ourselves what the *client* concept means.

When social workers ask themselves 'Who is the client?' they sometimes answer, 'This person' or 'That person'. But in some situations they may answer 'This group of people' or 'That group of people' or in other situations 'This community' or 'That community'. Because some clients are individuals not all clients are individuals. By the *client* we mean the *social worker's focus of interest and commitment*. The relationship with the client is always fundamental but this relationship is not always a relationship to an individual.

So the original question: 'Who is the client?' can now be rephrased as: 'Is the focus of interest or commitment for net-workers, a social field or a partnership? The answer is: 'Very rarely'. The only occasions when a client is likely to be a network or a partnership are when networking is undertaken within and on behalf of a closed group of some kind.

In a residential home for older people, the officer-in-charge might network with and on behalf of all the residents to facilitate new patterns of living involving more cooperation and collective activity.

So long as the work was entirely focused on the residents as a whole and their relationships with one another, we could say that the client was the community partnership. However, there are several circumstances which might change this.

One circumstance might be the need to network on behalf of the specific interests of specific groups of residents, not against the interests of others but rather to challenge disadvantage and discrimination within the home.

The isolated position of Black elders within a pre-dominantly White home might lead the officer-in-charge to network on their behalf. Networking would be undertaken with the residents as a whole but on behalf of Black residents.

It might still be appropriate to see the residents, as a whole, as a community partnership, because they will all need to be involved in any antiracist initiatives, but the primary focus of concern and commitment would at this time be the Black residents. If the work involved challenging racist stereotypes or confronting individual residents with the unacceptable nature of their behaviour, this distinction between client and community partnership would become very obvious.

Another circumstance which might create a distinction between clients and community partnerships would be the need to break down barriers between the home and the rest of the community. This would mean paying attention to the links residents had with family and friends (Douglas, 1986, p. 131) and the new relationships that might be established with people living outside the home in terms of shared interests. This would lead the officer-in-charge to assess opportunities for developing a wide range of links with a variety of individuals and organisations outside the home to develop an overlapping set of community partnerships serving the interests of the residents as a whole.

Differentiating between the concepts of *client* and *community partnership* solves one problem but creates another. If the client is not the community partnership or to be more precise is not the whole of the community partnership, then how do we go about identifying those others who might become members of this partnership?

Who should be included in a community partnership?

Networking always has a focus and therefore always relates either directly or indirectly to a client. This may be a person, a group of people, a client category, or a community. Identifying the client, enables us to see who should be part of the community partnership. This is not to say that we should always distinguish individual clients before we engage in any partnership work but we should always be able to relate the membership of a community partnership to the needs of the client. This is the only principle we need to guide us in our choice of partners.

In relation to HIV and AIDS there is a need to see community care in relation to *total support* leading to a model of 'flexible, augmentative social care planning' in which all 'social legal, health and interpersonal networks' could be included (Gaitley and Seed, 1989, p. 14). One interpretation of this is that professionals need an ability to link intensive relationship work with seriously ill people and their carers with the very different work that needs to be undertaken with consultants, hospital managers, home care organisers, etc. In this way, it has been argued, social workers, nurses and others will be able to grasp the pattern or *gestalt* of the total situation of a person living with HIV (Gaitley and Seed, 1989, p. 15).

John is about to leave hospital having partially recovered from a serious infection. He is able to move around with some difficulty but is breathless and easily tired. He wants to return home to his flat on a council estate where he lives alone. A former lover and some friends might be prepared to offer limited support. But there is little likelihood of family support as there has been no contact between him and his family since they discovered he was gay ten years before. Although some attempt could be made to reinvolve the family, its seems likely that much of the care needed will have to come from statutory and voluntary organisations. John is closely involved in the process of defining who should be involved as partners in the assessment process but on the whole, accepts advice he receives from the social worker.

In this case the assessment is undertaken in partnership with those who are likely to play a part in John's *care package*. Volunteers, a district nurse, the GP, a home help organiser, an occupational therapist, and a housing officer could work as an assessment partnership.

Much may depend on an effective inter-agency network to which managers will need to contribute. Links between health and social services are likely to be particularly important. This illustrates what can happen when there is little or no conflict between social worker and service user about the choice of partners.

But what if there were conflict and it was not possible to resolve it? What then? The answer has to be that if service users do not give permission for other people to be approached with a view to contributing to the assessment process, then, in the absence of any issues which might overide it — child abuse, evidence of mental illness, etc — this wish has to be respected. This may be particularly relevant to work with people living with HIV and AIDS[11].

What kind of information does network assessment produce?

In setting up and continuing to support a community partnership, we need both *hard* or objective information, and *soft* subjective information.

Hard information covers anything which might help us to understand the characteristics of a particular network mesh together with the likely effects of particular interventions. We are therefore likely to be interested in such things as: the pattern of interaction; the frequency of interaction; the role of brokers in linking together different parts of the network mesh; the way information flows around the system; and whether *action-sets* exist. As we are interested in facilitating community partnership, we are also likely to be interested in working out how specific interventions on our part might help to promote patterns of partnership in all these areas.

Soft information is as important as *hard* information. When the assessment task involves *joining* an existing social network, we may think of the networker as a 'controlled participant observer' (Moreno. 1978, p. 109) experiencing all the currents of thought and feeling flowing through that network. This kind of *soft* or *process* knowledge often plays a significant role in assessing what needs to be done to create a community partnership.

The home help/social worker liaisons mentioned previously were set up to address some of the process issues that emerged in meetings designed to gather information about the current state of home help/social worker communication. In one of these liaisons, a colleague and I attended a meeting which was characterised by much anger directed towards us as social workers. We were convinced that one of the issues which needed to be addressed by the liaison was the sense of being devalued and marginalised that home helps often experienced in their dealings with social workers. This helped us to create a partnership model which sought to overcome distrust through liaison meetings, regular referral opportunities, and an emphasis on joint work.

Another aspect of this concern with process is that it is potentially empowering. It is likely that many views and experiences effectively silenced by feelings of powerlessness will only be discovered, as in this example through reflecting on *process*. It is *process* which gives a voice to those who might otherwise not contribute to our understanding of a situation.

In any situation *hard* and *soft* information need to be combined in an integrated assessment.

How does an assessment partnership work?

It is impossible to lay down hard and fast rules about situations as varied as those described in this book, but the networking approach to assessment can be characterised in two ways as a process of

1. Integrating diverse perspectives to produce one multidimen-
   sional picture which can form the basis of any collective action
   undertaken by the partnership.
2. Continual feedback in the course of which the picture is constantly changed, either by:
   a. Extension: Filling in the assessment gaps as issues which are
      unclear at one point become clear later on; or by
   b. Transformation: Fundamentally rethinking our understanding
      of a situation.

The feedback process raises individual and collective awareness
and one consequence is that the networking approach to assessment is educational. When people begin to build up a picture of
how things are now and how they might be different in the
future, they are educating and empowering themselves.

This may become clearer if we contrast the networking
approach with the traditional approach.

A traditional referral to a Social Services Department often takes
the form of a request for a particular service and the traditional
response is to assess people in terms of whether they qualify for
this service or not. This is hardly an empowering experience for
the client as the power to give, lies with the professional. In
contrast a networking response begins to challenge this imbalance
of power by working with clients and current members of their
networks to analyse existing situations and speculate about the
future. This process could be defined as working towards an
understanding of what the problems are and how new resources
could be liberated by changes in the way in which network
members relate to one another or changes in the composition of
the network. Key networking questions are: 'Who would be
prepared to do what?' and, 'How helpful would it be, anyway?'
They can only be answered in a framework of negotiation and
partnership associated with choice and empowerment. This raises
the issue of partnership contracts.

How do we contract with a community partnership?

Partnership contracts must relate to and be congruent with
contracts made between social workers and clients. If there are
conflicts between the contracts made between members of a community partnership and those made between social workers and
clients, then this would suggest there might be serious problems
with the networking approach. In fact, this problem is more apparent than real. This is because we are not comparing like with like.

We have to remind ourselves that a community partnership is a relatively open-ended structure composed of a number of particular patterns of interaction. All its members thus have a special relationship with it and need a specific contract with it. The partnership contract is the sum total of all these contracts including the contract between social worker and client. It does not exist separately except as a statement about how all the specific undertakings can contribute to the aims and objectives of the contract made between the social worker and the client.

Any community partnership is the product of a number of specific negotiations and the more complex the partnership, the less likely is it that all those involved will directly negotiate with one another. In situations like this the partnership contract may well be an abstraction. Nevertheless, it will be important as it will contain the overall rationale of the community partnership. We can illustrate this in relation to the complex partnerships currently being developed for people living with and affected by HIV and AIDS.

People living with HIV and AIDS have a number of interdependent medical and social needs. Some can only be met by liaising and contracting with hospital based staff. Others can only be met by liaising and contracting with neighbours, friends, family, and community based services such as home helps and district nurses. Wherever they are based, social workers need to address the whole range of medical/social, hospital/community issues. Hospital based social workers may have a particular concern with medical networks within the hospital but they also need to address the formal and informal networks which will support the client *in the community*.

Only if these networks are functioning well will it be possible to discharge the patient/client from hospital. Likewise, patch based social workers and home care organisers may be concerned with developing localised, *interwoven* networks of care. They will need to acknowledge the significance of the medical network which links their client to specialist hospital based services and find ways to relate to this network, particularly when the client is in hospital.

One of the major obstacles to effective liaison and collaboration in the field of HIV is the gulf that often exists between hospital and *community* based services. The need to hand over responsibility to another professional as soon as a person becomes ill or gets better is particularly inapporprite. For example in the case of HIV and AIDS there is a pattern of frequent sudden deteriorations in health followed by periods of at least partial remission. One way of addressing the need for the partnership contract to be made in both places simultaneously might be by creating teams based in both the hospital and the community. Some experiments on these lines are now being made[12]. In the future one might hope that such teams could assist in the spinning of a complex web of inter-agency relationships to plan the whole continuum of care from hospital to community.

HIV infection is associated with sudden and dramatic changes in health status. One of the reasons why community partnerships have to be negotiated with a wide range of people is to ensure that assessment and planning can be responsive to these changes. But even if less sudden, change is an issue whatever the problem or client group. Therefore, although network conferences and other events can help to facilitate the contracting process, contracting is best seen as a continuous process.

Summary

The networking approach to assessment is characterised by a concern with the relationship between needs and resources; the relationship between clients and community partnerships; and the relationship between the assessment process itself and the partnership principles which have been discussed in earlier chapters. Here are the questions which have been asked and the answers which have been given in this chapter.

1. *How do networkers discover needs?*
   They discover needs by engaging with community gatekeepers.
2. *How do networkers negotiate a communication network?*
   They do so by working in partnership with community gate-keepers of various kinds.
3. *Can there be an assessment if some of the partners are in conflict with one another?*
   Yes, but only if power is shared within the partnership. Alternatively, if the conflict stems from the attitudes of a powerful figure external to the partnership, the focus of the work will need to be changed so as to make the partnership inclusive of the conflict.
4. *Who is the client?*
   For a networker the client can be an individual, a group, or a community. The client is part of the community partnership but should be distinguished from it because the partnership exists to meet the needs of the client.
5. *Who should be included in a community partnership?*
   As many people or agencies as need to be involved in meeting the needs of the client.
6. *What kind of information does network assessment produce?*
   The networking approach to assessment generates both *hard* and *soft* data and combines them in an integrated fashion.

7. *How does an assessment partnership work?*
It is a process of continual feedback between members of the community partnership by which multiple perspectives are linked together and collective knowledge is either extended or from time-to-time transformed.

8. *How do we contract with a community partnership?*
A partnership contract is the sum total of all the separate but interdependent contracts made with all those involved in meeting the needs of the client. It is an axiom of partnership contracting that partners have a right to expect that they will get some of their needs met if they are to be enabled to meet the needs of others.

10 Networking with children and families

For professional social workers, networking is not just another social work method. It cannot be lightly picked up or put down. Reactions to it are rather extreme. To some it may seem rather trite and pointless. It is a long-term strategy in a world that increasingly asks social workers to produce instant results so ensuring that it will not be universally popular. Moreover, the skills that it requires are exercised in decidedly unglamorous ways, often over months or years. The more effective it is, the less likely it is that many people will notice it has been going on: networkers defuse crises; promote mutual understanding; and encourage cooperation and collaboration. None of this is very newsworthy and nobody ever got famous by being involved in it. But, on the other hand, networking is immensely flexible and adaptable and, if we allow it to permeate our practice it can make almost everything we do a little bit different.

This chapter will explore the consequences of a permeative approach to networking and it will do so in terms of one particular client group: children and families. The rationale for this is that social work is becoming increasingly specialised and most social workers, now see their work in terms of a particular client group. If this is the context in which networkers will operate then it will be helpful to show how networking might permeate a specialist client group.

Work with children and families is selected not because this client group is seen as having any special priority, but because, in many ways, it represents a *test case* for the networking or community partnership approach. It is the branch of social work which has become most identified with *law and order* issues and most preoccupied with the individual rather than the community. Therefore if networking can offer a set of useful practice frameworks for child care workers it seems likely that it will have something to offer those working with other clients groups, as well.

Child abuse

This topic increasingly dominates the lives of a large part of the social work profession and can define the public image of social work, and to a lesser extent, the image that social workers have of themselves.

The networking approach to child abuse has implications for every aspect of child protection work.

Investigation

An investigation of suspected child abuse could be seen as an attempt to discover whether or not, a child's personal network is an abusive field, ie a field of relationships in which abuse has been able to or could flourish. This is not just a question of the general level of family support although this may tell us something about the probability of abuse (Garbarino, 1976, pp. 178–85). We need to know if there are specific risk factors present in a child's personal network. Also whether some parts of this personal network could contribute to a protective partnership in which a number of professionals may also need to be involved.

We saw in chapter one, how an approach which adopts a social network perspective moves us away from standardised notions of the family. In terms of child abuse, the social network perspective is therefore child centred rather than parent centred[13]. It does not make assumptions about the location of abuse nor the location of protection and support. The strongest argument for this is that we can never know in advance where these lie.

In addition to parents, teachers, members of the extended family, neighbours, fathers of school friends, even social workers may all be potential abusers. In one situation in which I was involved as a social worker, it was discovered that a piano teacher was sexually abusing a number of children who went to him for lessons! In situations like this parents may be the key members of a protective partnership even if the abuse has occurred within the family. When it is revealed that a grandfather or uncle has been sexually abusing a child parents can act to prevent any further abuse occurring.

In other situations parents may be able to offer little protection because they are too implicated in the abuse themselves. Then the protective partnership may have to be based on other members of the extended family, neighbours, or even the parents of the child's friends. More commonly, it may be possible to include in the protective partnership one of the parents even if the other is the abuser.

If the investigation reveals that one or both parents have been abusing a child, it will often be possible to establish a protective

partnership which includes them provided they have acknowledged responsibility and shown a real wish to ensure that their
child is not exposed to any repetition of the abuse.

Prevention

We should never be concerned only with the detection of abuse
but equally with support and protection for a child on a continuous basis. This is likely to provide more genuine security for a
child than dramatic but intermittent interventions by social
workers, paediatricians, the police or anyone else. Networking
encourages a preventative approach to the question of child
abuse by focusing attention on the significance of a child's
personal social network.

The likelihood of abuse is increased if children do not have a
range of independent contacts with others who can exercise some
informal surveillance and if necessary intervene to protect them or
inform child protection agencies. The preventative approach is a
matter of reducing abusive opportunities and enabling children to
have people to whom they can turn if abuse occurs or if they are
frightened it might occur. Increased contacts between children
and protective members of their informal personal network can
often help, as can regular contact with a known and trusted
professional worker. Facilitating the growth of new relationships
by introducing children to clubs or IT projects where they will
make friends and meet responsible adults can also help to
prevent abuse occuring.

Children, themselves, wherever possible should be involved as
partners in any preventative strategy. After all, we are talking
about changes in a child's own personal network. Any changes in
whom they see or how often they see particular people or where
they have contact with them, must fit into a child's own sense of
who and what is significant in his or her social world. Failure to
attend to the child's eye view can lead to the child undermining
the very measures which are supposed to protect it. In the case of
sexual abuse, if a known paedophile is the only person to take an
interest in a child it will probably not be possible to prevent
contact unless the child's needs are recognised and work is done
with the child to develop other relationships to meet those needs.

Network abuse

One of the most extreme examples of a destructive and oppressive network is one linked to the organised sexual exploitation of
children. It has been alleged that some of this exploitation involves *ritual abuse*.

In the case of so called *ritual abuse* or any other form of
organised abuse, the abusive network may be able to create its

own very powerful legitimating norms which can silence children (Furniss, 1991, pp. 329–30). It can militate against any of the abusers *breaking ranks* and providing information about what is going on (Observer, 1990). Anyone involved in the abusive network who may want to *confess* is likely to come under extreme pressure from other members of the network not to do so in case they are in turn implicated.

There are therefore very powerful mechanisms keeping an abusive network intact. Ignoring the existence of the abusive network and concentrating on an individual abuser and victim, may leave this source of oppression untouched and reduce the chances of helping even known victims — let alone unknown ones. It will do little to protect future victims of the network.

In this connection, it may be that networking has something to offer. Direct work with the abusive network as a whole is neither possible nor appropriate. But work with all those who have experienced abuse and their families — a network of the abused — can help to encourage children to talk about their experiences (Furniss, 1991, pp. 329–30). Such an approach might be seen as an attempt to establish an empowering network capable of challenging the oppressive power of the abusive network.

Another complementary approach might be to attempt to work with individual abusers to encourage them to talk about the abusive network. This would amount to an indirect network assessment. If an abuser is showing signs of wanting to cooperate, it may be possible to gain information about how the network operates. The aim of such an indirect assessment would be in the first instance, to discover ways of counteracting the pressures towards secrecy emanating from the network and to challenge the role the network might play in the abuser's own defensiveness and refusal to take responsibility. If abusers tend to have weak ego strength and a consequent tendency to avoid reality (Furniss, 1991, p. 34) then this can only add to the power the abusive network has over the individual abuser. A knowledge of how conventional and respectable networks maintain their own norms, communicate informally, and mark their boundaries with secrets might be used to understand and ultimately counteract this power.

Networking may also play a part in the preventative work undertaken with abusers both in the *community* and in prison.

At least two factors maintaining abusive behaviour could be connected with the relationship between the sexual abuser and his social network. Fear of losing his network of family and friends may prevent an abuser from fully accepting what he has done. Moreover, especially in prison, abusers may find that the only people willing to accept them are other abusers who may collude in denying the seriousness of what, they have done. In prison segregation and persecution of *sex offenders* of all kinds may reinforce the solidarity of collusive networks and lead them to cling even more firmly to the idea that they are victims rather than perpetrators. Although reliable information on this subject is notoriously difficult to discover, the high levels of reoffending characteristic of convicted sex offenders (Finkelhor and Associates, 1986, p. 130–223) might be explicable in network terms.

To counteract the tendency for sexual abusers to form isolated and collusive networks an analysis of how these networks could be normalised through desegregation in the prison system would be beneficial both to *sex offenders* and to society as a whole. Alongside work with *sex offenders* it may be possible to undertake work with other inmates and prison officers on the role that sex offender mythology has in maintaining defensive macho norms in the rest of prison. But a much more thorough study of these questions is needed before specific networking strategies could be recommended.

In relation to abusive networks, networking is the mirror image of its usual self. The aim is to loosen ties rather than strengthen them. However, this sort of work needs to go hand-in-hand with the building of empowering networks for those who have been abused themselves, or directly affected by abuse. There is a need to encourage the development of new social networks either in prison or out of it to enable *sex offenders* to help one another resist their own inclinations and pressure from others to once more get involved in sexual abuse, either as individuals or as members of a network. There is a need for professionals to stay in much closer contact with *sex offenders* on their release from prison than is usual to offer a mix of practical advice, support, and to monitor their behaviour. Such strategies would help to build a preventative community partnership.

Professional network

Certain groups of professionals are invariably involved in child protection issues. Police, paediatricians, social workers, health visitors, teachers and others form a professional child protection network. There is a need to work closely together and yet the high anxiety levels associated with this type of work can make it very difficult to foster trust and cooperation (Furniss, 1991, pp. 59–113).

All too often conflicts which might be manageable in another context prove to be unmanageable in relation to child protection. For example, the breakdown in the relationship between the police and the local authority in Cleveland seems to have been a major factor in the collapse of public confidence in child protection services in that county. There have been numerous occasions when as a key worker in a child abuse case I found myself in conflict with social workers, health visitors, teachers and others. However, I also found that a better level of mutual understanding could almost always resolve these conflicts.

The lesson I continually learnt as a practising social worker was that collaboration in such a controversial and painful area of decision making as child abuse does not work unless the ground has been prepared by some form of inter-agency liaison. Sometimes the results of an effective liaison could be dramatic.

The Head Teacher of a local primary school was beginning to exasperate local social workers by her tendency to overreact to indications of possible child abuse. Numerous, inappropriate conferences were called which not only wasted valuable professional time but also damaged the confidence of parents in education, health and social services. A regular meeting between a Social Work Team Manager and the Head Teacher was able to resolve this problem very quickly. It transpired that opportunities for a discussion about the range of services provided by the local authority and the possibility of informal contact to discuss possible referrals were all that was needed.

Case management of child protection

Inter-agency networking may pave the way to better mutual understanding between professionals, but there is also a need for the orchestration of child protection services around the needs of particular children. In a sense the chair of a child protection conference is a case manager who has a responsibility for facilitating service planning as well as decision making.

As a case management tool, child protection conferences could be seen as doing much more than registering and deregistering children. Through the conference new services could be brokered and *interwoven* with existing services in care and protection *packages*. On a day-to-day basis many of these case management functions could devolve to the *key worker*. This person, usually a social worker would then be the main *packager* of care and protection, linking members of the inter-agency network with one another and members of the informal network.

Child protection conferences could be seen as the main vehicle for involving parents and other people who might be important to the child in the process of decision making. As far as parents are concerned, inviting them to attend conferences and to participate in service planning, creates opportunities for negotiating the part they would be expected to play in making the *package* work. Conference decisions could provide a framework for this because they could be seen as a partnership contract which committed everyone to working together in a particular way.

Networking explicitly addresses these case management and brokerage functions. If widely adopted it would lead to service planning meetings as an integral part of child protection work and in general better *team work*.

Support for parents

The parents of abused children often feel very alone with their problems. Fear of other people's reactions may prevent them from talking about their feelings and experiences. Various attempts have been made to facilitate the development of support networks for abusive or potentially abusive parents (Starr, 1982, pp. 48–49). In my experience Family Centres can perform an invaluable function by introducing these families to one another. Providing opportunities for this to happen could be seen as networking to promote the development of a community of interest among these parents.

Where parents have felt themselves to be the victims of an injustice they have sometimes been able to use their links with each other to launch a campaign for an inquiry: as in the case of the Cleveland Inquiry into sexual abuse investigations in the county. This kind of activity is an important check on professional power and should be encouraged rather than discouraged by social workers whatever the rights and wrongs of the particular case. If there is a concern as in Cleveland, that only one part of the case is being put then the response should be to provide opportunities for other *communities of interest* such as incest survivors to mobilise themselves. In this way it may be possible to ensure that inquiries and subsequent reviews of policy take all points of view into account.

Child protection: the community approach

These are some examples of the kind of networking activity which can be systematically developed in relation to child protection issues. Child abuse acts as the focal point around which all this networking activity is generated and any one worker could be in touch with a number of separate community partnerships simultaneously. Together all these partnerships form an interdependent whole involving a very wide range of people and helping to relocate child abuse as a community problem rather than thinking of it simply as a family problem.

Looking after children

For some time, it has been clear that when a child leaves home and enters the care system, 'insufficient attention is given to the exploration of kin and neighbourhood networks as potential sources of support' (Packman, 1986, p. 203). A networking approach would try to help the child sustain these relationships and moreover involve those who demonstrate a commitment to the child in the process of child care planning.

Partnership in planning

There is currently a movement towards a greater partnership with parents in childcare planning and this movement is likely to be accelerated by recent UK legislation. A networking approach implies broadening the range of planning *partners* to include all significant other adults. This means that the significant members of a child's network should be represented at statutory reviews or if this presents problems at less formal meetings. If successful this would ensure that when children return home they do not return only to their parents but to at least some of their other previous relationships. Also, this would reduce the likelihood of parents and children spending too long in each other's company in the first few crucial weeks when family tensions may reemerge and blow the family apart once again. Field social workers, foster parents, and residential social workers can all contribute to this kind of networking.

Building a child centred network

Professionals involved in child care spend much of their time on communicating with a variety of other professionals.

> It is not unusual for example, to find a local authority field social worker regularly telephoning an IT unit, a solicitor and residential staff on behalf of one boy who is in the care of the local authority; whilst telephoning teachers and educational psychologists about his younger brother; and telephoning the housing department to get essential repairs done to the family home. Very often this work although of great importance is seen as a distraction from the *real* work. It can certainly be very frustrating.

For all concerned it is vital to go beyond isolated, fragmented and often hostile communication with one another, if an integrated mesh of resources around children and families is to be created.

Liaisons between health visitors, social workers, family centres, volunteer centres, housing workers, schools, doctors, etc form an essential backdrop to the creation of specific partnership arrangements. Often these liaisons can be created with a relatively modest investment of time and energy.

Liaison structure can be used to mobilise an *action-set* appropriate to the needs of a particular child. This process of mobilising professional *action-sets* is a case management style response to the needs of children. This kind of model applied to the complex family example given above might lead to the creation of several overlapping action sets each focusing on a particular child or alternatively one large multipurpose network dividing into different *action-sets* to tackle different family issues. If the social worker were the case manager he or she might find that they were spending less time trying to explain one professional's views to another and more time facilitating flexible patterns of collaboration.

Joint working

A recognition that field and residential workers, foster parents and others all form part of the child or young person's support network naturally leads to various forms of collaborative activity including pieces of joint work. For example it may be appropriate to use a children's home as a venue for a series of family interviews conducted by a residential social worker and a field social worker as part of preparing for a young person to return home.

Self-help

Another aspect of a child's support network is peer support. In the case of children in residential or foster care, these kind of links should be encouraged by professionals.

Children in the care system often feel devalued and stigmatised. The National Association of Young People In Care has drawn attention to this (Stein and Ellis 1983) as part of its work as a self-help organisation which is based on a network of contacts between those who have recently left care and those still in the care system. Encouraging young people to participate in self-help networks helps to empower a very disadvantaged part of our society.

Networking with young people leaving care

It has to be recognised that those who have been in care for a prolonged period of time in many cases do not return to live with their parents. When they leave care at 17 or 18 years age they cannot simply pick up precare relationships where they left off many years before. For these young people a major need is for some help in negotiating the transition to *independence*.

It has been strongly argued that the traditional idea of *training for independence* fails to recognise the frequent need for a quite prolonged phase when young people need access to flexible forms of support (Stein and Carey, 1986, pp. 153–68). Following from this a number of projects have been developed which are modelled on a type of network.

In one case 16–17 year olds who are in care are placed with local families who are supported by project workers based in a youth club. This club also provides a *normal*, unstigmatising social centre for the young people concerned and continues to fulfil this function when they move into their own *follow on accommodation*. Through the club young people are given access to a number of overlapping peer support networks. In their *follow on accommodation* they are visited by a project worker who acts as a source of informal advice and support. It is planned that young people will move on to their own permanent accommodation when they are ready.

This project recognises the central role played in the transition to adult life by flexible support network providing both continuity and change. It attempts to provide this for the young people coming to it. Moreover the *foster* families are also provided with opportunities for professional and mutual support and the project itself is a result of a collaborative link between a Social Services Department and the project. Moreover the project networks locally to glean additional assistance, for example printing is done by a local school.

The whole project is a good example of networking in a number of related fields simultaneously to ensure that one form of networking supports another. It relies on active networking by a number of people including foster parents, local authority field social workers, youth club workers, housing support workers and the young people themselves[14].

Summary

Networking is either a permeative approach or it is nothing. As it permeates practice it opens up a whole range of possibilities for community partnership. Moreover, as social workers and others become involved in the process of community partnership, we have seen how they begin to assume pivotal roles in helping to integrate a wide range of activities and partnerships with one another. In this way, the brokering of individual community partnerships inevitably leads to systems brokerage. Here, the focus was on two issues around which partnership systems might grow: child abuse and children and young people living away from home and being *looked after* in residential or foster care.

In relation to child abuse, networking was shown to lead to a distinctive approach to a number of issues:

1. Investigation was characterised by a concern with the analysis of a child's personal network in terms of both risk factors and partnership possibilities.

2. Prevention was characterised by a process of building on existing supportive relationships in a child's personal network and where necessary working with children and young people to make changes in the personal network. This might involve seeing less of some people and more of others; or it might involve making use of opportunities for meeting with new people; or it might involve all of these things.

3. Responses to network abuse and the more general issue of working with abusers were characterised by a range of strategies to help children who have been abused, their families, and individual sexual abusers to challenge or escape from the collusive or threatening power of the abusive network.

4. Professional networks are often permanently locked in conflict or mutual misunderstanding. Interprofessional networking was seen as being able to overcome these problems through the processes of liaison and collaboration.

5. The case management of child abuse by child protection conferences was seen as a way of effectively coordinating services, whilst involving parents and others close to a child in the decision making process. In particular, it was shown how a set of conference decisions could be seen as defining the terms of a partnership contract to which all those involved would be committed.

6. Support for parents was seen as a vital aspect of child protection work characterised by providing opportunities for mutual support which could enable parents to face up to their responsibilities for abuse and empower them to challenge *the system* if they felt they had not been dealt with fairly by it.

In relation to children and young people *looked after* by local authorities, networking was shown to likewise have the potential for a very general impact on practice.

1. Networking can help to prevent children being *lost in care* by helping them to maintain contact with friends and family whilst living away from them.
2. Networking can help to extend the partnership concept beyond parents to other significant adults.
3. Networking can lead to a child centred practice which can help to overcome interprofessional conflicts.
4. Networking can encourage joint work and other forms of collaboration which can make more effective use of scarce resources.
5. Networking can facilitate children and young people in their attempts to join with one another for the purposes of self-advocacy.
6. Networking can help to create the kind of many layered partnerships which young people leaving care require involving young people themselves, their peers, foster parents, residential workers, statutory and voluntary agencies.

Conclusion

Networking approach to community partnership

Networking is a way of thinking about social work as well as a method of doing it. It is a way of thinking about needs in terms of situations; and a way of thinking about situations in terms of more or less complex patterns of interaction, communication and exchange. If networking sometimes seems difficult to define it is not only because it has grown up in a higgledy-piggledy fashion but because it is a betwixt-and-between practice which can only be found outside the formal institutional structures of the Welfare State. It is not easy to stick a label on what networkers do because they work with relatively open-ended *social fields*, in which the challenge is always to build partnership and community out of difference and sometimes conflict.

And yet, in spite of this, it is not impossible to analyse the skills and strategies involved in the networking approach to community partnership and this is what I have set out to do.

The key to an understanding of networking is the way in which it defines community partnership as a certain kind of social network. At a practice level this means that networkers are concerned with issues such as:

- Type and level of contact members of a community partnership have with one another;
- Accessibility of needs in relation to resources within a particular pattern of network interaction;
- Roles played by brokers in linking the different parts of a network together and therefore either facilitating or blocking the development of partnership;
- The formation of networks of empowerment; and
- Link between community partnership and the presence of at least some degree of reciprocity within a network exchange system.

Generalised network awareness can, in itself, offer valuable insights into how individuals and groups can be helped to get their needs met through network sensitive interventions of various kinds. But networking involves more than just a willingness to take account of and work through social networks. It involves applying network skills to the task of making and re-making community partnership. Community partnerships come in all

135

shapes and sizes but they are all social networks in which information, power and support are shared.

Unfortunately, networks in which partnership occurs naturally are quite rare. Networking is an attempt to self-consciously promote patterns of sharing by encouraging certain partnership processes to come to the fore.

It is an enabling strategy which is concerned with:

1. Interpersonal relationships and in particular the way in which key individuals relate to one another;
2. Community as a source of self-identification and as a process of empowerment and mutual support,
3. Flexible and informal as opposed to bureaucratised and institutionalised ways of relating to other people,
4. Communication processes for sharing information and establishing a shared network culture,
5. Action-sets and the strategies involved in mobilising them.

At any one time networkers may focus more on some of these processes than on others. But community partnership involves all of them. Having established this, we are then able to look at a number of community partnership practices in which networking plays a central role. This involves looking at some familiar things with different eyes and thus to some extent redefining them.

Varieties of community partnership

Patch social work is a community partnership practice characterised by a concern with strictly localised social networks with a shared commitment to and identification with the *neighbourhood*. Patch social workers are patch networkers. They search for ways of linking individuals, groups and agencies with one another. They try to help people to feel a part of the *neighbourhood:* to support one another and take collective action.

Patch social workers also operate in a deliberately casual style *dropping-in* on other agencies or on community groups. They adapt their role to suit the needs of the *local* community. This helps them to develop patchwide communication systems which raise the collective awareness of what is going on in the local area; paving the way for mobilising individuals, community groups, and locally based organisations in patch action-sets.

Inter-agency work is concerned with developing a different kind of community partnership — a partnership between agencies.

Inter-agency networkers seek out key individuals in other agencies and establish relationships with them. They work towards building mutual understanding between agencies and a sense of common purpose. They try to create opportunities for agencies and their representatives to actively support one another.

Inter-agency work involves encouraging what I have called a culture of innovation — a questioning of organisational traditions and a willingness to take a few risks. Setting up and maintaining inter-agency liaison structures is an essential part of this process. It can enable those who are part of a network of agencies to join with one another in inter-agency action-sets or collaborative endeavours.

Network therapy focuses specifically upon individuals, families and problems which are normally seen in *personal* terms. Network therapists are concerned with the interplay between *personal* problems, the dynamics of network relationships, and what key individuals can offer one another. They try to promote the idea of the personal network as a *community* — something with which people can identify, and through which they can feel supported and empowered.

All this can only be done if networkers are able to *start from where the network is* and work with the situation as they find it. Network therapy involves straightening out distorted communication so increasing the general flow of information around the network system. Ultimately network therapy involves network action to solve network problems. Network therapists have a role in coordinating the process by which individuals come together in problem solving action-sets.

Case management shares with network therapy a concern with the individual and his or her support system. It differs in that the focus is less on the family and more on ways of coordinating formal support services. Case managers work with the intricacies of dependence and autonomy and how this affects relationships between those involved in making a *care package* as effective as possible. They promote a sense of collective responsibility and a team identity. Through this both formal and informal carers may overcome feelings of isolation and obtain support and help in getting their own needs met.

Case management involves a continuum of activities each appropriate for a different kind of situation. Case managers are permanently engaged in redefining their roles to operate a *needs-led* service. Effective communication in the context of clear guidelines about confidentiality is a vital aspect of case management. Case managers should take a lead role in establishing and maintaining communication systems, to effectively negotiate the basis of network collaboration.

Self-help differs from other forms of networking in that the initiative should rest principally with members of the self-help network. This does not mean that professionals have no role to play: they need to beware of being so *helpful* that they undermine the efforts of the self-help network. Effective self-help involves mutual acceptance. Sometimes this may not be immediately forthcoming and will have to be worked for. Social workers and others may be able to contribute to this process culminating in the development of a sense of community with concrete opportunities for mutual support and collective action.

Once a community is established it is important that those who continue to feel isolated are helped to join. Again, social workers and other professionals may be able to help people to join self-help networks. They can also help these networks to resist the temptation to become over-formalised or too amenable to the needs of professionals and the State. Communication is essential if a self-help network is to sustain itself. Professionals can offer useful practical help with the production of newsletters, the holding of meetings, etc. In all this social workers need to appreciate, however that self-help networks do not conveniently compartmentalise their activities: when self-helpers come together it may be as much for campaigning as mutual support.

Networkers as community brokers

Although all the partnership practices listed above have their strengths we have also exposed some of the problems that can arise. Patch social work finds it difficult to come to terms with partnerships not seen in local terms. Inter-agency work needs to base itself on what service users are saying — not just on what makes life easier for the agencies. Network therapy needs to be disentangled from a certain naivety about the extended family. Case management is much more complex than current discussions about implementing a *care market* might indicate. Self-help networking needs to take account of the fact that people may choose to identify themselves in a whole range of different ways: thus no self-help community can develop without some planning and negotiation.

I have tried to show that these problems can be overcome if community partnerships are seen as mutually supportive of one another rather than as mutually exclusive of one another. This rests on the proposition that there are certain things which they all share. It goes beyond the question of the nature of community partnership and concerns the role which networkers consistently play as they enable partnership to emerge and be sustained.

Networkers are community brokers. They act as mediators or makers of channels of contact, communication, and collaboration. This means that they plan and invest in their relationships with those who might enable them to access partnership in the future. They resolve conflicts based upon misunderstanding and help to promote the value of change and manage its consequences for those involved in community partnership. Their approach is holistic and concerned not just with specific problems but the context in which these problems exist. They are aware that within any community partnership there may be very different views or interpretations about the nature both of these problems and the basis of the partnership: they are prepared to help to explain the community partnership to itself. Finally, it means that networkers try to avoid monopolising channels of contact and communication. They see their role in terms of power-sharing.

By acting as a community broker, networkers tend to develop chains of practice which are also chains of partnership. They develop a range of mutually supportive community partnerships around a central issue or problem. Thus the role of community broker takes on a new meaning: that of mediator between partnership networks, rather than just within a particular partnership network. At this level, community partnership becomes systems brokerage and need not be thought of only in terms of what one person does. Several people and several agencies spread over a period of time may participate in systems brokerage, a macro-level process, by which various aspects of a system are brought into alignment with one another. Community care was used as an example of how systems brokerage could help to integrate inter-dependent systems which might otherwise fragment.

Implications of a networking approach
Having argued that an integrated approach to networking is possible. Some of the implications have been explored. In relation to assessment, it was possible to answer a number of questions raised by this approach highlighting the significance of:

1. Engaging with community gatekeepers;
2. Negotiating a communication network;
3. Addressing sources of conflict within a potential partnership network;
4. Identifying the client and differentiating between clients and network;
5. Defining the scope of the potential partnership;
6. Synthesising the information received;
7. Seeing assessment as a process of continuing reappraisal in the context of continuous feedback; and
8. Contracting with the members of a community partnership.

Finally, having considered some of the assessment implications, we looked at the difference a networking practice oriented to community partnership might make to those working with a particular *client group* if it permeated all aspects of the work. Work with children and families was selected as a test case.

We saw how networking might affect both the investigation and the prevention of child abuse and how it might have a particular relevance in the case of network abuse. We also saw how the concept of the professional network might help to promote interdisciplinary teamwork and the case management of child protection. The network approach might also lead to parents of abused children being offered opportunities to overcome their own stigma and isolation.

For those concerned with *looking after* children on behalf of the State, we saw how a networking approach would encourage a child centred practice and new forms of partnership with families and other professionals. This would facilitate planning for those leaving home and those returning home or moving out of the care system to live independently. It would open possibilities of working simultaneously through a number of mutually supportive partnership networks.

New professionalism

One of the distinctive features of networking is that the position of the networker is necessarily ambiguous. The networker is a *participant observer*: a member of a wide range of networks and yet never fully identified with any of them. Networkers have to engage with members of a particular network. Yet if they are to retain their ability to facilitate, they cannot afford to be totally identified with them. Getting the balance right between *participation* and *observation* is perhaps one of the most difficult things about networking. The skills required to do this are perhaps the core skills of what is emerging as a new definition of professionalism.

There are two features of the welfare scene which stand out as we move towards the year 2000. Firstly, people are no longer prepared to be passive consumers of standardised services. We need a new concept of welfare citizenship and new welfare methodologies if these expectations are to be met. Secondly, inter-agency collaboration is now a fact of life for all those involved in health, education and the personal social services. The boundaries between professions are beginning to be much more permeable than in the past: some boundaries are breaking down altogether. Networking helps to redefine professionalism in the contexts of both demand for welfare citizenship and the growth of inter-agency work and multi-disciplinary teamwork.

Networking can contribute to the growth of welfare citizenship as an *empowering* strategy

● Specifying welfare as a partnership between service providers and service users rather than something which is done by service providers to service users;
● Enabling people to come together around shared experiences of oppression and develop the strength to challenge that oppression;
● Demystifying the nature of professionalism and redefining it as an enabling process;
● Promoting inter-agency and multidisciplinary work.

Community care, child protection, community health work all require inter-agency and interdisciplinary collaboration between statutory and non-statutory agencies, and between social workers, nurses, community workers and others. But in the absence of a shared language and a model for thinking about work with each other, good intentions are likely to founder on the rocks of mutual incomprehension. Networking opens up the possibility of creating a language and a model for cooperation and collaboration.

If welfare agencies are going to be actively involved in networking it is not only practitioners who will have to learn new skills. It is also managers. They will be actively involved in establishing inter-agency partnerships and links with users' groups. They will need to learn how to stimulate and evaluate networking initiatives; also how to supervise and support networkers. They will need to come to terms with the fact that networking subverts the traditional practitioner/manager dichotomy by emphasising the management aspects of practice and the practice aspects of management! Managers like practitioners may need to reinvent their role.

This book began by referring to a vision of community partnership which stimulated the evolution of networking as a social work practice. The paradox is that although this vision is very important and in some quarters may even seem revolutionary, it is also, very modest. Whereas theories like Psychoanalysis or Marxism make sweeping claims about human nature; the laws of the mind or the laws of history: networking remains cheerfully agnostic on these matters. It requires of those who want to practice it, no great *leap of faith*, only a stubborn belief in the ability of people to find strength, purpose, and power in and through their relationships with others.

Some may feel that this kind of pragmatic idealism offers an insufficient basis for good practice. My hope is that those who have become healthily suspicious of any form of determinism may have found in this book sufficient support for the basic social work principle: that however isolated or oppressed individuals and groups may be they need not be entirely powerless in the face of the apparently monolithic structures of the State, or the workings of the Market.

Whilst it would be foolish to pretend that all human problems can be solved though social networks. It is nonetheless true that social network perspectives open up a range of perhaps uniquely flexible, open-ended, supportive and empowering strategies which seem well suited to the demands of our time.

Notes

1. This was reported to me by Andy Brown, a community worker in London Borough of Hammersmith and Fulham.
2. Whenever I have talked about networking at conferences or in seminars, these two issues have been raised.
3. Gregory Bateson, polymath and founding father of family therapy, argued that information is pattern recognition (Bateson, 1973, pp. 382–383).
4. The Staffordshire *Pin Down* scandal is a good example of an abusive regime which went unchallenged because of the dominant culture in residential home for children in that county.
5. This definition of partnership is based on some comments by Sheila Macdonald in the course of a training session on the *1989 Children Act* in September 1991 at the West London Institute of Higher Education.
6. Personal Communications from Justine Pepperrell, formerly of Women's Health Network and Clive Turner, former patch team leader in the London Borough of Hammersmith and Fulham and now HIV and AIDS Programme Coordinator at CCETSW.
7, 8 and 9. I am grateful to Suneel Chadha for this information.
10. Network analysis is a technique which can be learnt (*See* for example Seed P., 1990). This does not in itself constitute a community partnership practice. Network analysis is one among many techniques which can be made use of by networkers.
11. These issues are explored in With Both Eyes Open. *Social Work Today* Vol. 23 14, 28th November 1991 14–15 by Fenella Trevillion.
12. For example in the London Borough of Hammersmith and Fulham.
13. For this insight I am grateful to a comment made by Professor Jean Lafontaine at a conference *Assembling Human Knowledge to solve Human Problems* at University of York, March 1990.
14. Based on information supplied by Alison Partridge, researcher, Oxfordshire Social Services.

References

Abrams P 1980 Social Change, social networks and neighbourhood care. *Social Work Service*. 22nd February 12–23

Abrams P, Abrams S, Humphrey R, and Snaith R 1989 *Neighbourhood Care and Social Policy*. London HMSO

Adams R (1990) *Self-Help, Social Work and Empowerment*. Basingstoke, Macmillan

Alperin DE, Richie ND 1989 Community Based AIDS Service Organisations: challenges and educational preparation. *Health and Social Work*. Vol. 14 **3** August 165–173

Adler S 1987 Models of care in the Hospital and the Community. In Williams S ed. *Caring for People with AIDS in the Community. Report of a conference held at the Institute of Education, University of London, 25th March 1987* London King Edward's Hospital Fund for London 11–13

Auslander GK Litwin H 1987 The Parameters of Network Intervention: A Social Work Application. *Social Services Review*. Vol. 61 **2** June 305–18

Auslander GK Litwin H 1988 Social networks and the Poor: toward effective policy and practice. *Social Work*. 33 **3** May–June 234–38

Austin CD 1983 Case Management in Long-Term Care: Options and Opportunities. *Health and Social Work*. Vol 8 **1** 16–30

Bakker B Karel, M 1983 Self Help Wolf or Lamb? in Pancoast D, Parker P, Froland C (eds) *Re-discovering Self Help*. Sage Publications 159–81

Ballard R, Rosser P 1979 Social Network Assembly. In Brandon D, Jordan B (eds.) *Creative Social Work*. Oxford Basil Blackwell 69–84

Bamford T 1990 quoted in Care Management — what does the future hold? A one day seminar organised by SWT *Social Work Today*. Vol 21 **42** 8–9

Barclay PM 1982 *Social Workers: their role and tasks*. London NTSW Bedford Square Press

Barnes JA 1954 Class and Committees in a Norwegian Island Parish. *Human Relations*. **7** 39–58

Barnes JA 1969 Networks and Political Process. In Mitchell JC (ed.) *Social Networks in Urban Situations: analyses of personal relationships in Central African towns*. Manchester Manchester University Press 51–76

Bateson G 1973 Cybernetic Explanation. In *Steps to an Ecology of Mind*. London Paladin Books Granada Publishing.

Bayley MJ 1973 *Mental Handicap and Community Care: a study of mentally handicapped people in Sheffield*. London Routledge and Kegan Paul

Bayley MJ 1978 *Community Oriented Systems of Care*. Berkhamsted The Volunteer Centre

Bebbington A, Warren P 1988 *AIDS: the local authority response*. Canterbury PSSRU University Kent

Bennett B 1980 The Sub-office: A Team Approach to Local Authority Fieldwork Practice. In Brake M, Bailey R, (eds.) *Radical Social Work and Practice.* London, Edward, Arnold 155–181.

Bennett R 1980 *Ageing, Isolation and Resocialisation.* London Van Nostrand Reinhold Company

Bennington J 1970 Community Development Project. *Social Work Today.* Vol 1 **5** p. 5

Benson JE 1987 *Working More Creatively with Groups.* London Tavistock

Beresford P, Croft S 1980 *Community Control of Social Services Departments.* London Battersea Community Action

Beresford P, Croft S 1986 *Whose Welfare: Private Care or Public Services?.* Brighton Lewis Cohen Urban Studies Brighton Polytechnic

Body Positive. 1990 Newsletter **102** 25th September

Bott E 1971 *Family and Social Network: roles, norms and external relationships in ordinary urban families.* London Tavistock

British Association of Social Workers 1980 *Clients are Fellow Citizens: Report of the Working Party on Client Participation in Social Work.* Birmingham, BASW Publications

Broderick CB 1988 Healing Members and Relationships in the Intimate Network. In Milardo RM (ed.) *Families and Social Networks.* London Sage 221–34

Bulmer M 1987 *The Social Basis of Community Care* London, Unwin Hyman

Butler-Sloss E 1988 *Report of an Inquiry into Child Abuse in Cleveland 1987.* London, HMSO (Cm. 412)

Caplan G 1974 *Support Systems and Community Mental Health: lectures on concept development.* New York, Behavioural Publications

Children Act 1989 London, HMSO

Children Act 1989 ch 41 London, HMSO

Collins AH Pancoast DL 1976 *Natural Helping Networks: A Strategy* National Association of Social Workers

Collins J 1989 Power and Community Care; implications of the Griffiths Report. *British Association for Social Anthropology in Policy and Practice.* Newsletter **4** 12

Cooper A 1989 Neighbourhood and Network: a Model from Practice. In Darvill G, Smale G, (eds.) *) Partners in Empowerment: Networks of Innovation in Social Work.* London, PADE NISW

Cooper A, Pitts J 1989 Getting Back to Normality — Anti-Racism, Anti-Sexism and After. Paper presented to the Second Biennial Seminar on Theoretical Concepts and their Relationship to the Curriculum organised by the European Regional Group of the International Association of Schools of Social Work Bled Yugosalvia

Cooper M 1980 Normanton: Interweaving Social Work and the Community. Hadley R, McGrath M (eds.) *Going Local: Neighbourhood Social Services* 29–40, London, NCVO Occasional Paper 1, Bedford Square Press.

Croft, S and Beresford, P (1989) User–Involvement, citizenship and Social Policy. *Critical Social Policy* 26 9 No 2 5–18

Currie R, Parrott B 1986 *A Unitary Approach to Social Work — Application in Practice* Birmingham BASW

Day PR 1988 Social Networks and Social Work Practice. *Practice*. vol 2 **3** 269–84

DOH 1989 *Caring for People: Community Care in the Next Decade and Beyond* Cm 849 London HMSO

DOH 1991a *Care Management and Assessment: Managers Guide*, London HMSO

DOH 1991b *Care Management and Assessment: Summary of Practice Guidance* London HMSO

Dominelli L 1988 *Anti-Racist Social Work.* Practical Social Work. London Macmillan

Dominelli L, McLeod E 1989 *Feminist Social Work.* London Macmillan

Douglas T 1986 *Group Living: the application of group dynamics in residential settings.* London Tavistock

Dourado P 1990 American Dreams Come True. *Social Work Today.* Vol. 21 **25** 16–17

Drennan V 1988 *Health Visitors and Groups: Politics and Practice.* London Heinemann

Edwards R 1988 Issues for Community Projects Developing Local Involvement. In Henderson P (ed.) *Working with Communities.* London The Children's Society 29–43

Ellis J 1989 *Breaking New Ground* London Bedford Square.

Emerson AR 1982 *The Glaven District Caring Committee: final report.* University of East Anglia School of Economic and Social Studies mimeo

Epstein AL 1969 Gossip, Norms and Social Network in Mitchell JC (ed.) *Social Networks in Urban Situations: analyses of personal relationships in Central African Towns.* Manchester, Manchester University Press 117–27

Finkelhor D et al 1986 *A Sourcebook on Child Sexual Abuse* London Sage

Fitzpatrick R, Boulton M, Hart G 1989 Gay Men's Sexual behaviour in Response to AIDS — insights and problems. In Aggleton P, Hart G, Davies P (eds.) *AIDS: social representations, social practices.* London, The Falmer Press 127–46

Froland C, Pancoast DL, Chapman NJ and Kemboko, PJ 1981 Linking Formal and Informal Support Systems. In Gottlieb (ed.) *Social Network and Social Support.* London, Sage, 259–75

Foucault M 1979 *Discipline and punish; the birth of the prison.* Harmondsworth, Penguin

Furniss T 1991 *The Multi-Professional Handbook of Child Sexual Abuse: Integrated Management, Therapy and Legal Intervention.* London Routledge

Gaitley, Seed P 1989 *HIV and AIDS: a social network approach.* London Jessica Kingsley

Garbarino JG 1976 Some ecological correlates of child abuse: the impact of socioeconomic stress. *Child Development.* **47** 178–85

Garbarino J 1983 Social Support Networks: Rx for the Helping Professions. In Whittaker JK Garbarino J (eds.) *Social Support Networks: Informal Helping in the Social Services.* New York Aldine 3–28

Garbarino JG 1986 Where does Social Support Fit into Optimizing Human Development and Preventing Dysfunction? *BJSW* **16** Supplement 23–37

Gay P 1983 Action Learning and Organisational Change. In Peddlar M (ed.) *Action Learning in Practice*. London Gower 153–64

Gittins D 1985 *The Family in question: changing households and familiar ideologies*. London Macmillan

Goffman E 1968 *Asylums: essays on the social situation of mental patients and other inmates*. Harmondsworth Penguin

Greif GL, Porembski E 1988 AIDS and Significant Others: findings from a preliminary exploration of needs. *Health and Social Work*. Vol. 13 **4** Fall 259–65

Griffiths R 1989 *Community Care: Agenda for Action*, London HMSO

Grant G and Wenger C 1983 Patterns of Partnership: three models of care for the elderly. In Pancoast D, Parker P, Froland C *Rediscovering Self Help*. Sage Publications 27–51

Hadley R McGrath M 1980 *Going Local: neighbourhood social services*. London Allen and Unwin

Hadley R, Cooper M, Stacy G 1987 *A Community Social Worker's Handbook*. London Tavistock

Hall R 1988 The Inter-Agency Approach. In Henderson P (ed.) *Working With Communities*. London The Children's Society 82–92

Hedley R 1984 *Neighbourhood Care in Practice*. Neighbourhood Care Action Programme

Hedley R 1985 *People in Networks: managing a neighbourhood care group*. Neighbourhood Care Action Programme

Hewitt R 1986 Community Mental Handicap Teams: service provision and linkage strategies. In Grant G, Humphreys S, McGrath M (ed.) *Community Mental Handicap Teams: theory and practice*. BIMH Conference Series British Institute of Mental Handicap

Hicks C 1988 *Who Cares: looking after people at home*, London Virago

Hill M 1982 Professions in Community Care in Walker A (ed.) *Community Care: the Family the State and Social Policy*. Oxford Basil Blackwell Martin Robertson 56–75

Holman B 1983 *Resourceful Friends: Skills in Community Social Work*. London, Children's Society

Humphreys S, McGrath M 1986 Community Mental Handicap Teams: problems and possibilities. In Grant G, Humphries S, McGrath M (eds.) *Community Mental Handicap Teams: theory and practice*. BIMH conference series London British Institute of Mental Handicap 21–37

Hunter DJ, Wistow G 1987 *Community Care in Britain*: variations on a theme. London King Edward's Hospital Fund for London

Jordan B 1990 *Social Work in an Unjust Society*. London Harvester Wheatsheaf

Kleizkowski BM, Elling RH, Smith DL 1984 *Health System Support for Primary Health Care*. Geneva World Health Organisation

Laming H 1989 Meet the Challenge. *Community Care* August **3**

Laing RD 1965 *The Divided Self*. London Penguin

Lindenfield G, Adams R 1984 *Problem Solving Through Self-Help Groups*. Ilkley Self-Help Associates

Maguire L 1983 *Understanding Social Networks*. London Sage

Maher P (ed.) 1987 *Child Abuse: the Educational Perspective* Oxford Basil Blackwell

Mantell JE, Shulman LC, Belmont MF, Spivak HB 1989 Social Workers Respond to the AIDS Epidemic in an Acute Care Hospital. *Health and Social Work*, Vol. 14 **1** February 41–51

Mayer AC 1962 System and Network: an approach to the study of political process in Dewar. In Madan C, Sarana G (eds.) *Indian Anthropology: essays in memory of DN Majundra*. Bombay Publishing House 266–78

Mayer AC 1966 The Significance of Quasi-Groups in the study of Complex Societies. In Banton M (ed.) *The Social Anthropology of Complex Societies*. ASA Monographs London Tavistock Publications 97–122

Milardo RM 1988 Families and Social Networks: an overview in Milardo RM (ed.) *Families and Social Networks* London Sage 13–47

Milson F 1974 *An Introduction to Community Work*. London Routledge and Kegan Paul

Mitchell JC 1969 The Concept and Use of Social Network. In JC Mitchell (ed.) *Social Networks in Urban situations: analyses of personal relationships in Central African towns*. Manchester Manchester University Press 1–50

Moreno JL 1978 *Who Shall Survive: Foundations of Group Psychotherapy and Sociodrama*. Beacon House New York

Murie A 1988 Housing, Homelessness and Social Work. In Becker S, and Macpherson S (eds.) *Public Issues, Private Pain: poverty, social work and social policy*. London Insight 262–70

National Health Service and Community Care Act 1990 London HMSO

National Youth Bureau 1988 *Windows on Practice: The Youth Service Response To AIDS* Leichester, NYB.

Observer 1990 Call for War Against Hidden Menace of Ritual Abuse. Sunday 16th September

Nissel M Bonnerjea L 1982 *Family Care of the Handicapped Elderly: Who Pays?* London Policy Studies Institute

Nutter S 1991 Doing it Her Way. *Social Work Today*, September 5th vol. 23 **2** 18–19

Oliver M 1990 *The Politics of Disablement* Basingstoke Macmillan

O'Malley J 1977 *The Politics of Community Action* Spokesman Books

Packman J 1986 *Who Needs Care: Social Work Decisions about Children*. Oxford Basil Blackwell

Payne M 1986a *Social Care in the Community* Basingstoke BASW/Macmillan

Payne M 1986b Community Connections through Voluntary Organisations: problems and issues. In Grant G, Humphreys S, and McGrath M, (eds.) *BIMH Conference Series* British Institute of Mental Handicap 60–77

Plant R 1974 *Community and Ideology; an essay in applied social philosophy* London Routledge and Kegan Paul

Rands M 1988 Changes in Social Networks Following Marital Separation and Divorce. In Milardo RM (ed.) *Families and Social Networks*. Sage, London 127–46

Reinhardt AM, Quinn P (eds.) 1973 *Family Centred Community Nursing: a socio-cultural framework*. Saint Louis, The C.V. Mosby Company

Robertson-Elliot F 1986 *The Family: change or continuity*. London, Macmillan

Rose SM, Black BL 1985 *Advocacy and Empowerment* London, Routledge and Kegan Paul

Ryan CC 1987 Statement of the Challenge. In Leukefeld CG, Fimbres (eds.) *Responding to AIDS: psycho-social initiatives.* Silver Spring, National Association of Social Workers 1–6

Schein EH 1985 *Organisational Culture and Leadership* London Jossey-Bass

Schumacher F 1974 *Small is Beautiful* Tonbridge Wells, Abacus

Seebohm Committee 1968 *Report of the Committee on Local Authority and Allied Personal Social Services* (Cmnd 3703, London, HMSO)

Seed P 1990 Introducing analysis in Social work. London Jessica Kingsley

SHAKTI Brochure on the south asian lesbian and gay network.

Smale G, Tuson G, Cooper M, Wardle M, Crosbie D 1988 *Community Social Work: a paradigm for change.* London, NISW

Social Work Today 17th October 1991 Vol. 23 **8** 18–19

Speck RV, Attneave CL 1973 *Family Networks.* Pantheon New York

Starr RH Jnr 1982 *Child Abuse Prediction: policy implications.* Cambridge Mass. Bollinger Publishing Company

Stein M, Ellies S 1983 *Gizza say?* National Association of Young People in Care

Stein M, Carey K 1986 *Leaving Care* Oxford Basil Blackwell

Steinberg RM, Carter GW 1984 *Case Management and the Elderly.* USA and Canada Lexington Books

Srinivas MN, Beteille A 1964 Networks in Indian Social Structure. *Man* **1xviv** 165–71

Taylor M 1983 *Resource centres for Community Groups.* London Community Projects Foundation and Calouste Gulbenkian Foundation

Taylor RDW, Huxley PJ, Johnson DAW 1984 The Role of Social Networks in the Maintenance of Schizophrenic Patients *BJSW* **14** 129–40

Toffler A 1971 *Future Shock.* London Pan Books

Trevillion F 1991 With Both Eyes Open. *Social Work Today* Vol 23 14 14–15

Trevillion S 1982 Welfare, Society and the Social Worker *BJSW* 12 **1** February 23–33

Trevillion S 1988 Conferencing the Crisis: the application of network models to social work practice. *BJSW* 18 **3** June 289–307

Vass A 1986 *AIDS a Plague in US: A Social Perspective — the condition and its Social Consequences.* St Ives Venus Academica

Wagner G 1988 *Residential Care: A Positive Choice* Report of the Independent Review of Residential Care London HMSO

Weber M 1978 *Economy and Society.* Roth G, Wittich C (eds.) London University of California Press

Warren DI 1981 *Helping Networks: how people cope with problems in the urban community.*

Whittaker JK 1986 Integrating Formal aand Informal Care: a conceptual framework. *BJSW* **16** Supplement 39–62

Williams MR 1985 *Neighbourhood Organisations: seeds of a new urban life.* Greenwood Press

Wiseman T 1989 Marginalised Groups and Health Education About HIV Infection and AIDS. In Aggleton P, Hart G, Davies P (eds.) *AIDS: social representations, social practices.* London The Falmer Press 211–19

Youth Clubs 1989 **152**

Index